Rooted in WACKY FUN PART 2

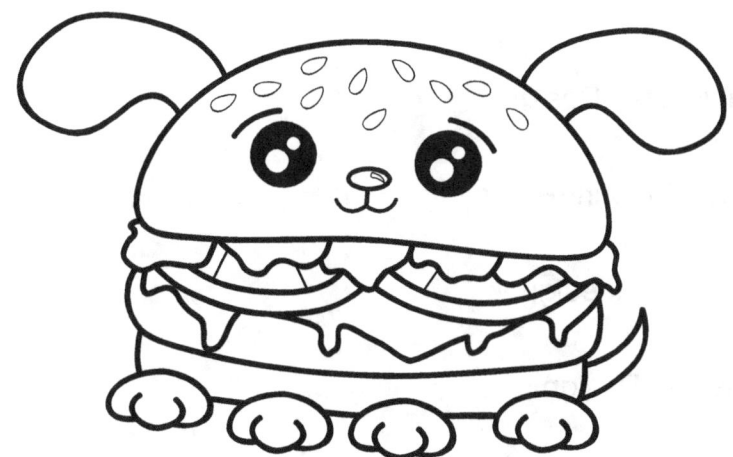

A coloring adventure for all

Jeanette Wummel

Coloring Tip:

When coloring with markers place a piece of paper between pages to prevent bleeding to your next design.

Acknowledgments

I can never say thank you enough to all the people who have supported and encouraged me in making my dreams come true. I would like to give a big thank you to my fans. I love hearing from you all. You all inspire me and make me want to keep creating! Keep being awesome!

I also want to thank Sal Gonzalez, Shelly Pfeiffer, Shelly Davis, Teresa Stafford, Tine Louise Eintzen, and her daughter, Mille for helping to come up with some of the designs that made it into the book. You are all great!

Follow me

Website/Blog:
www.TheRootsofDesign.com

Facebook:
www.facebook.com/TheRootsofDesign

Facebook Group:
www.facebook.com/group/ColoringRoots

Instagram:
www.instagram.com/therootsofdesign

Twitter:
https://twitter.com/Roots_Of_Design

Etsy:
www.RootsDesign.Etsy.com

Patreon:
www.patreon.com/RootsOfDesign

Copyright

Published and Manufactured in the United States
www.TheRootsOfDesign.com

Designs: Jeanette Wummel

ISBN-10:0-9982152-2-8
ISBN-13:978-0-9982152-2-8

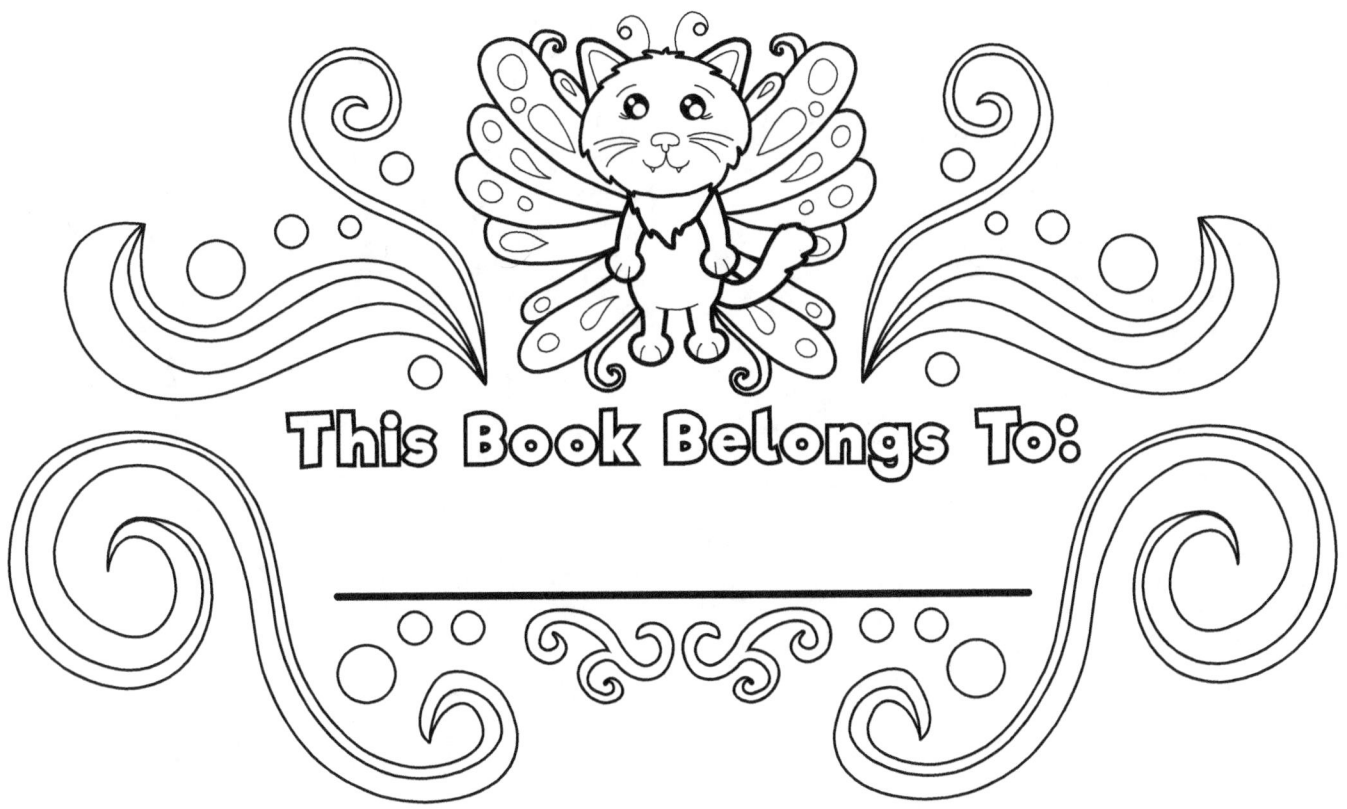

This Book Belongs To:

_____

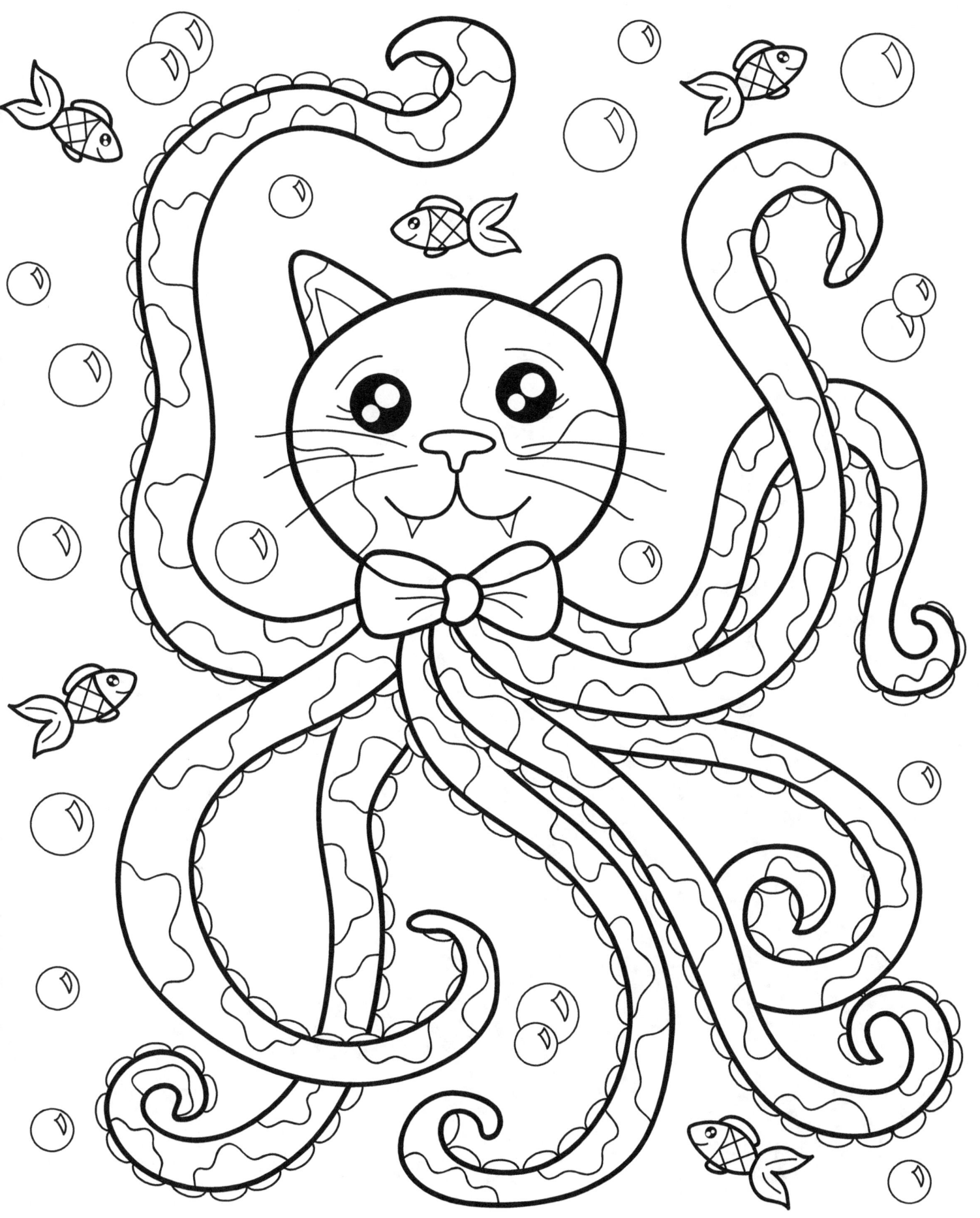

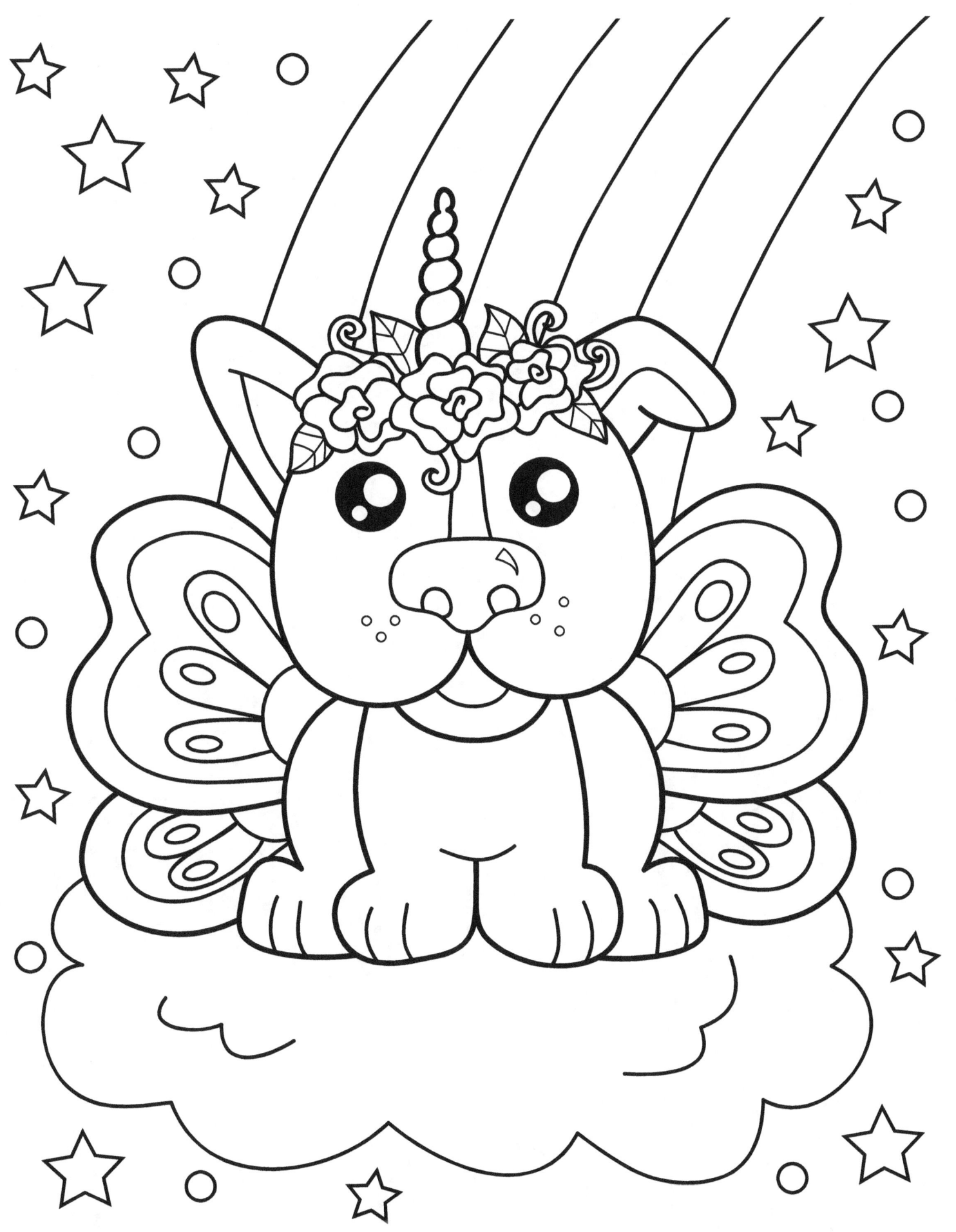

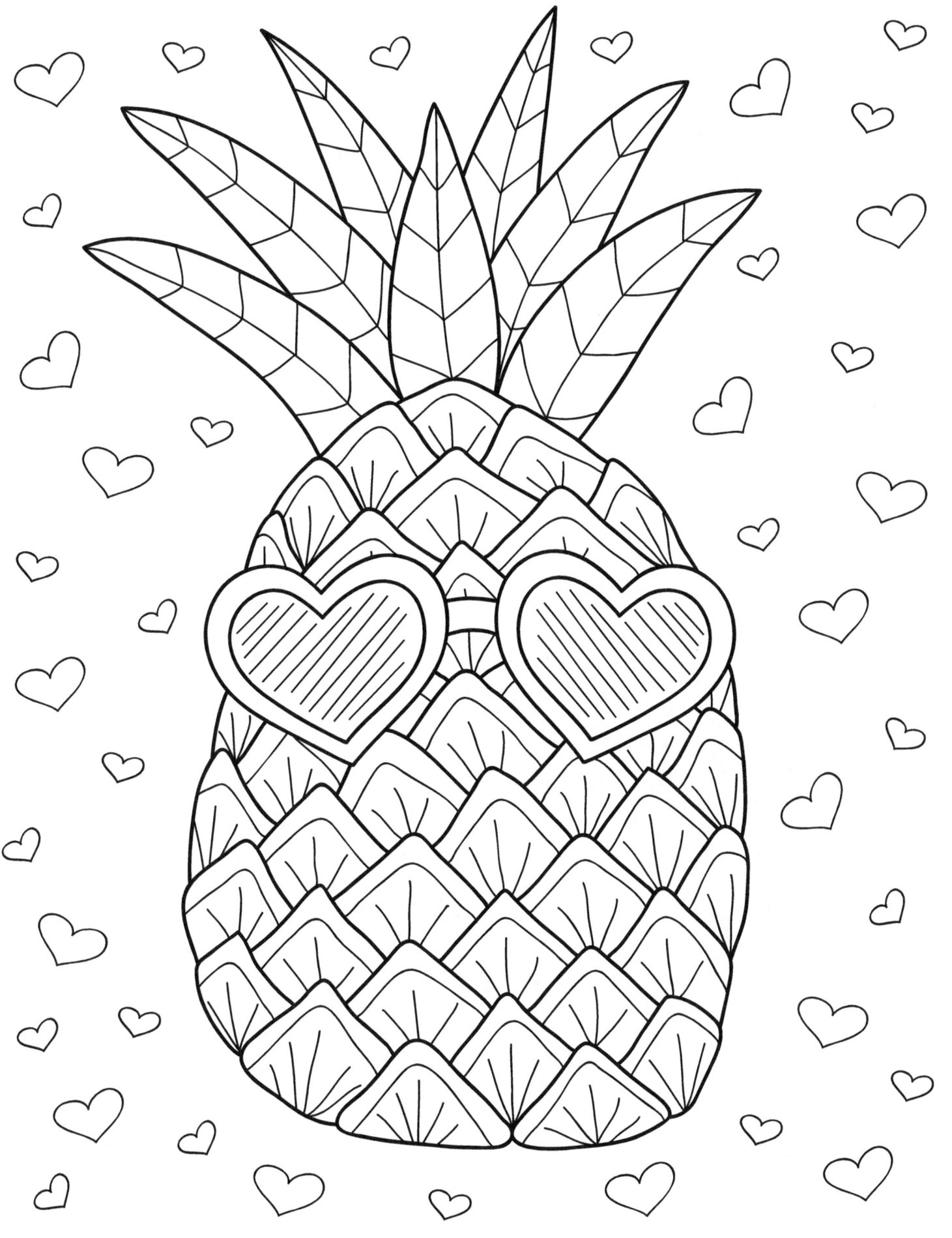

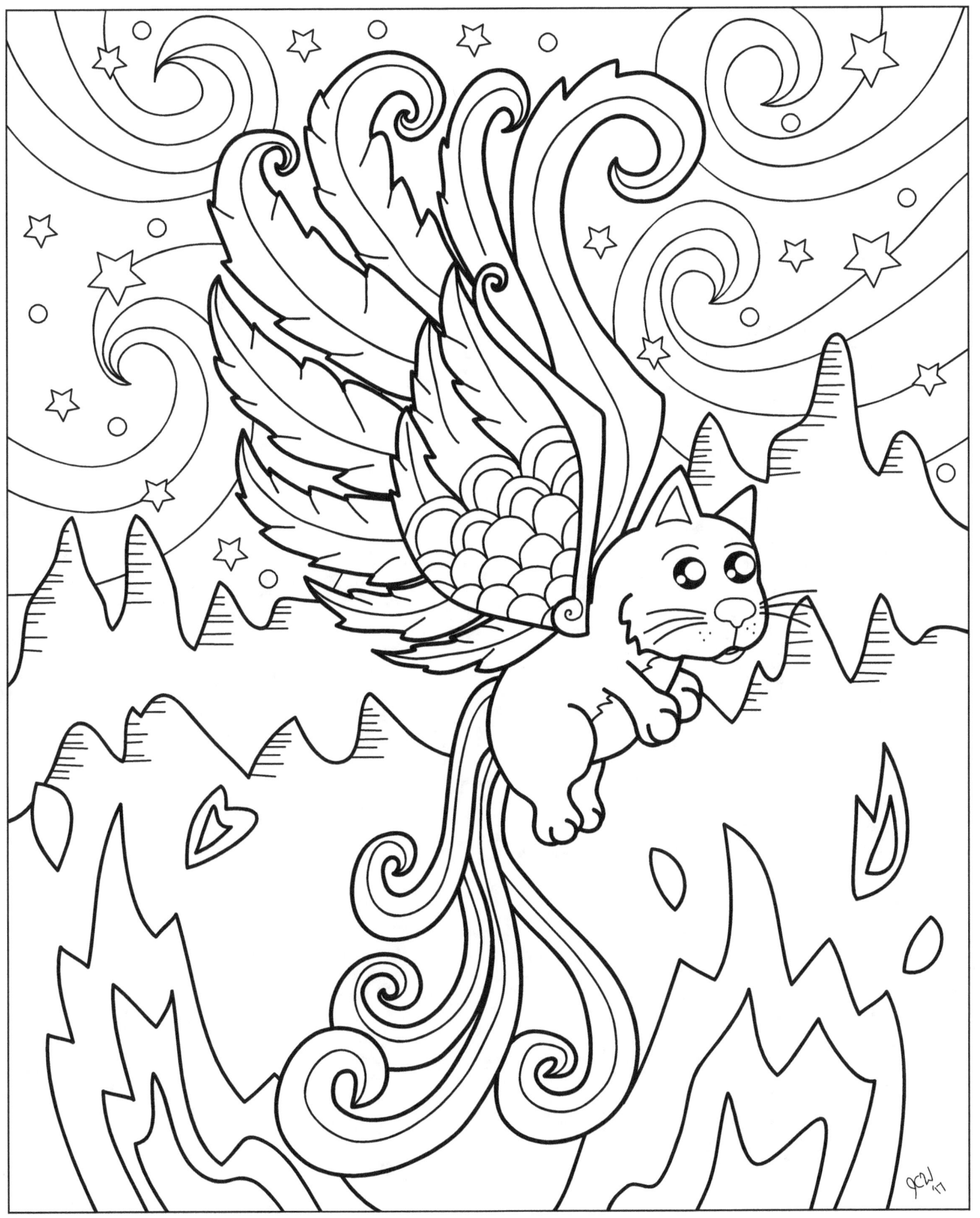

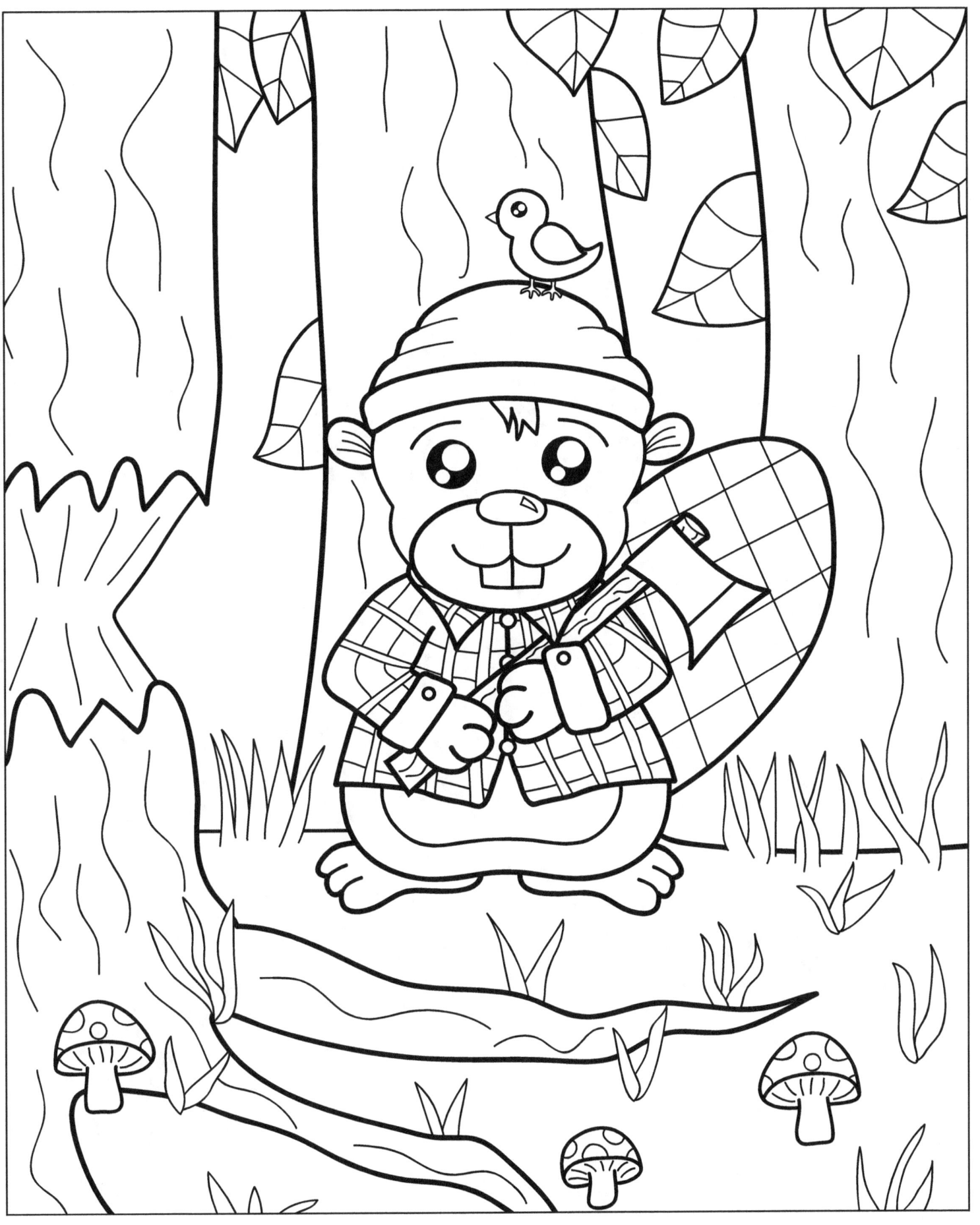

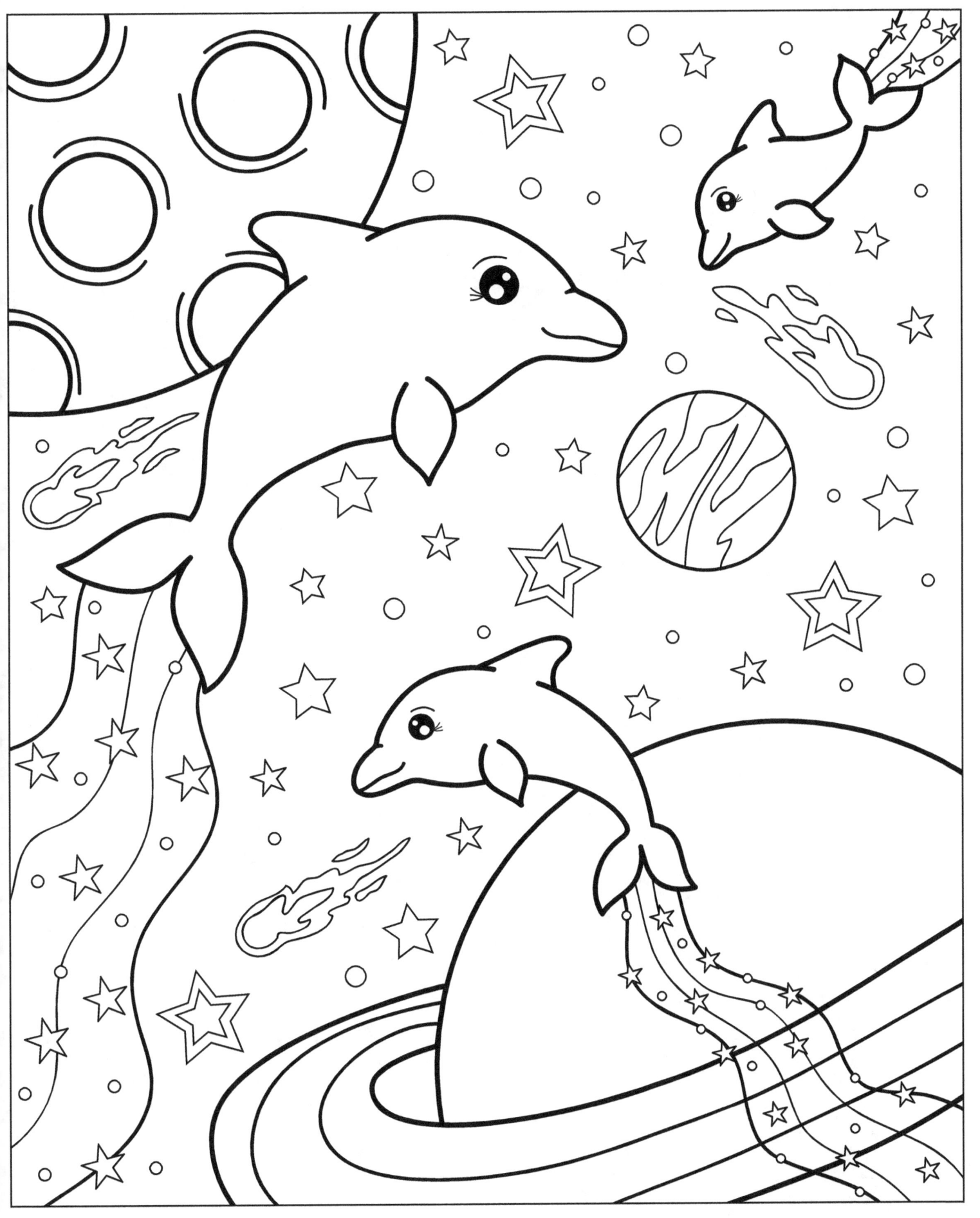

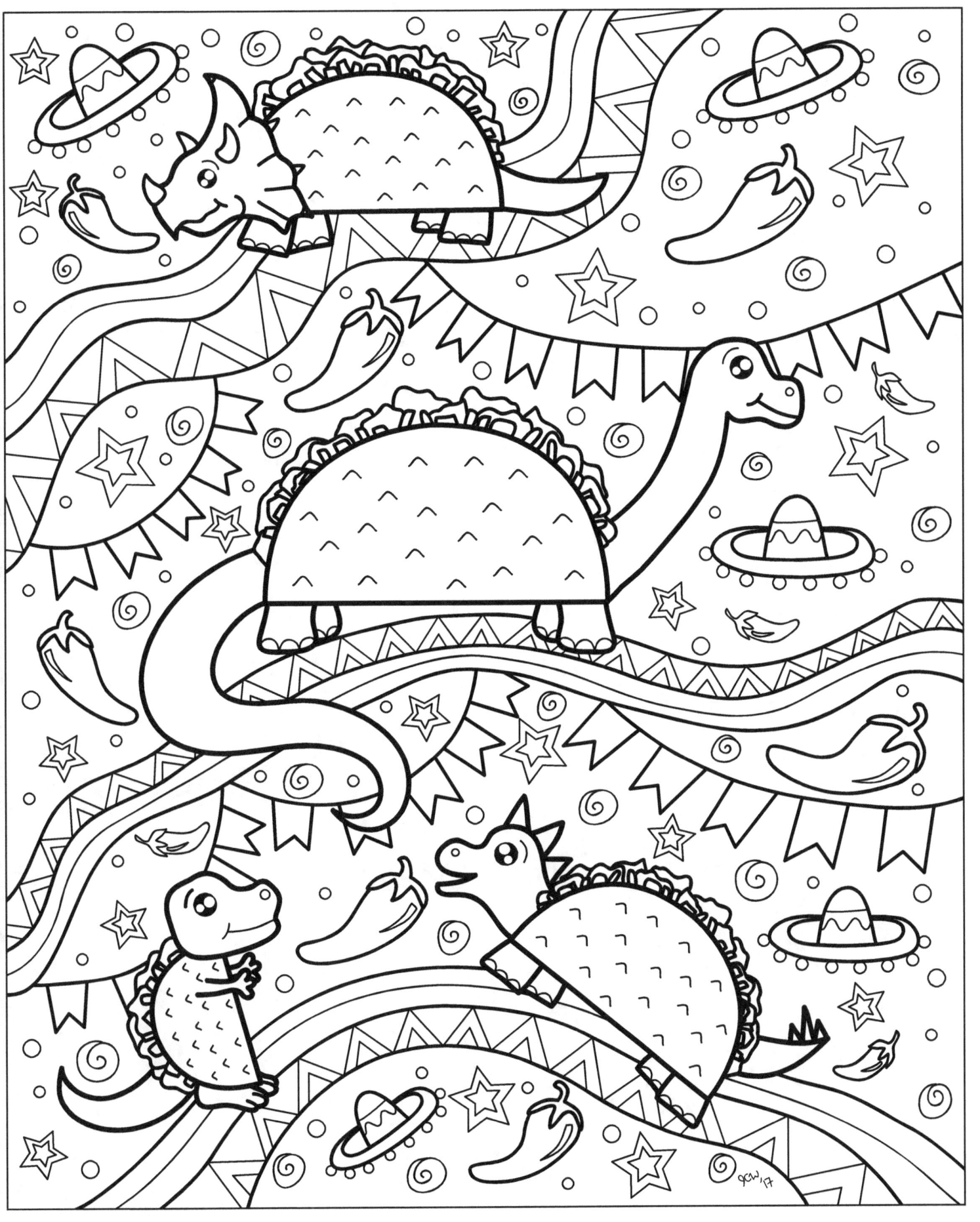

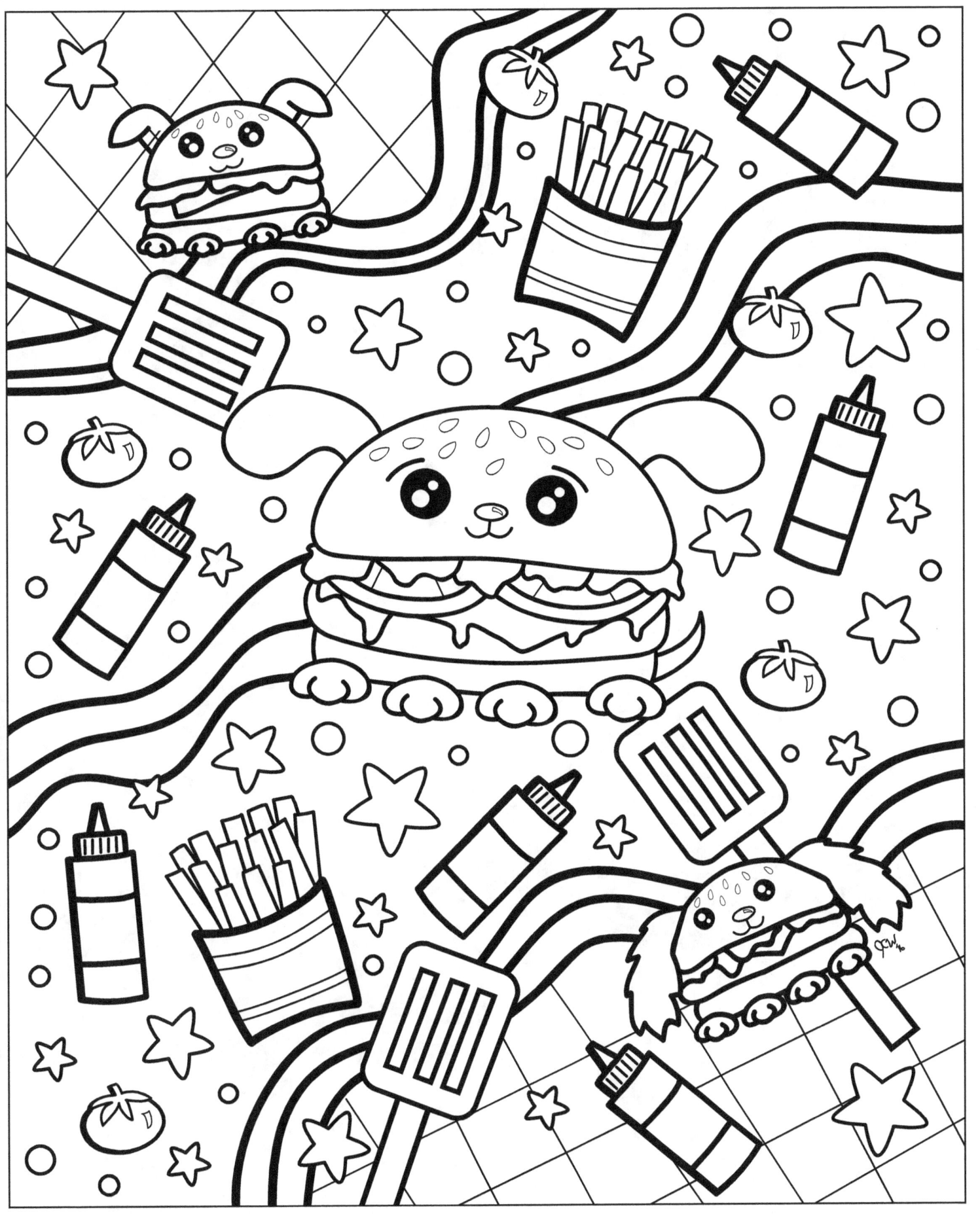

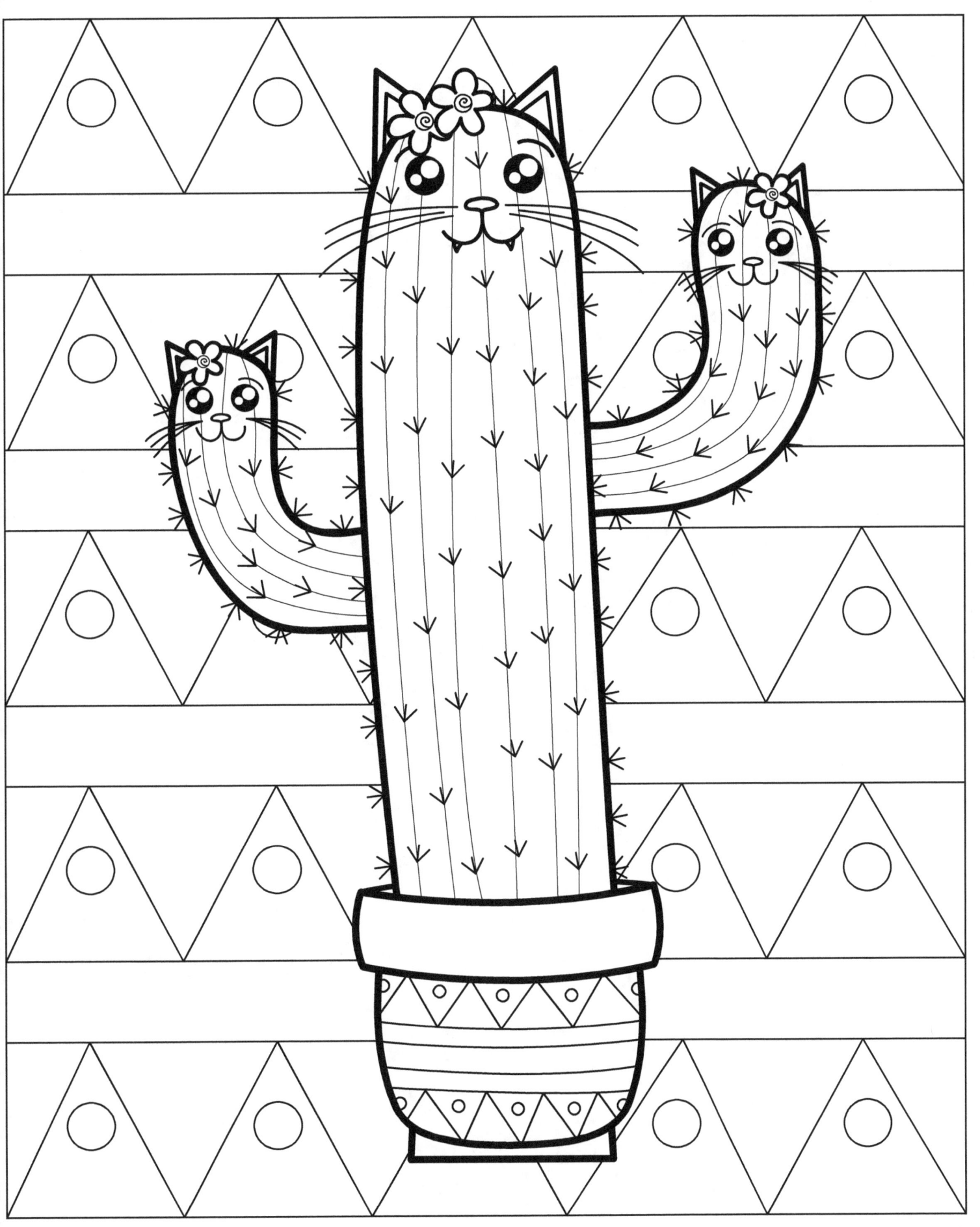

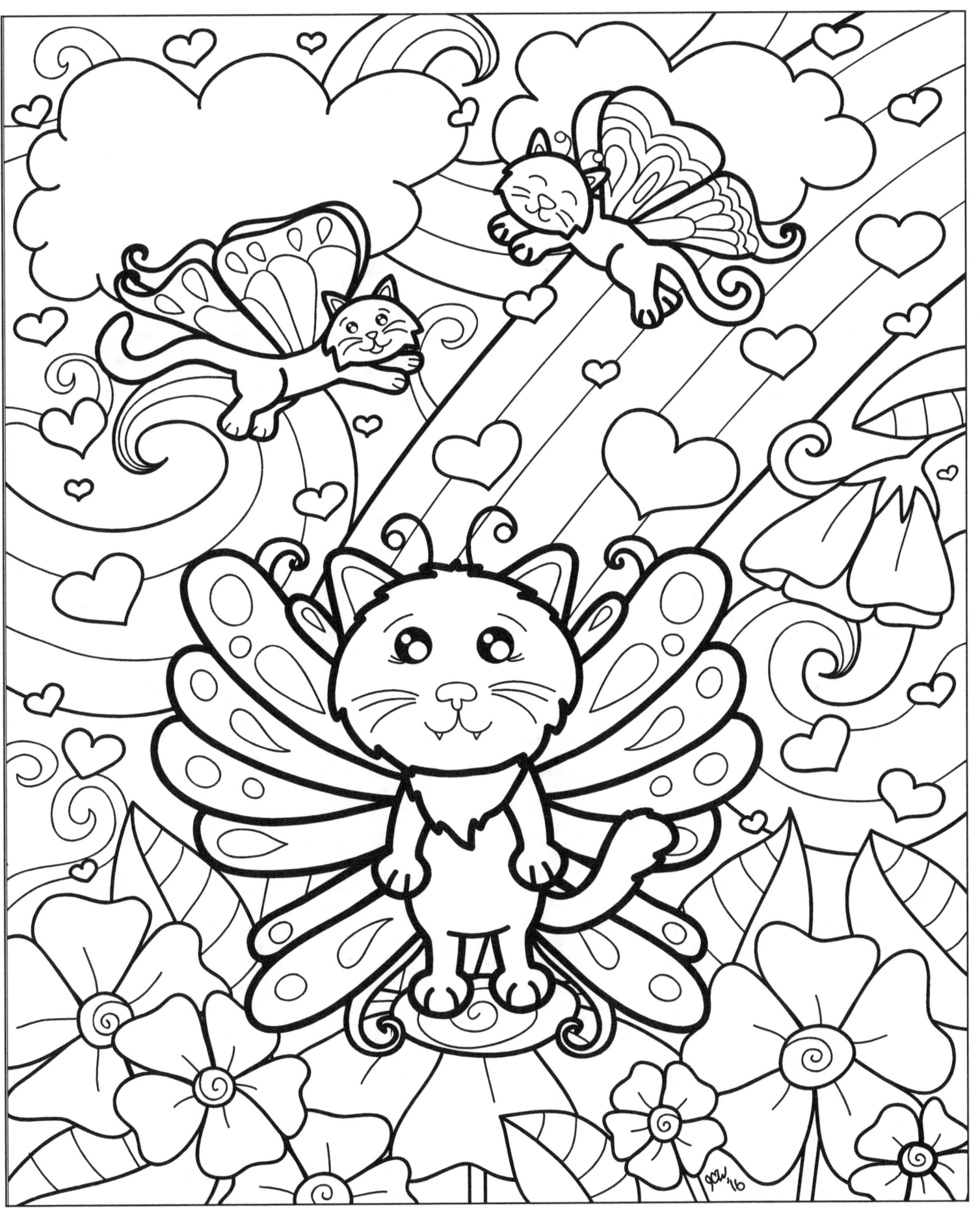

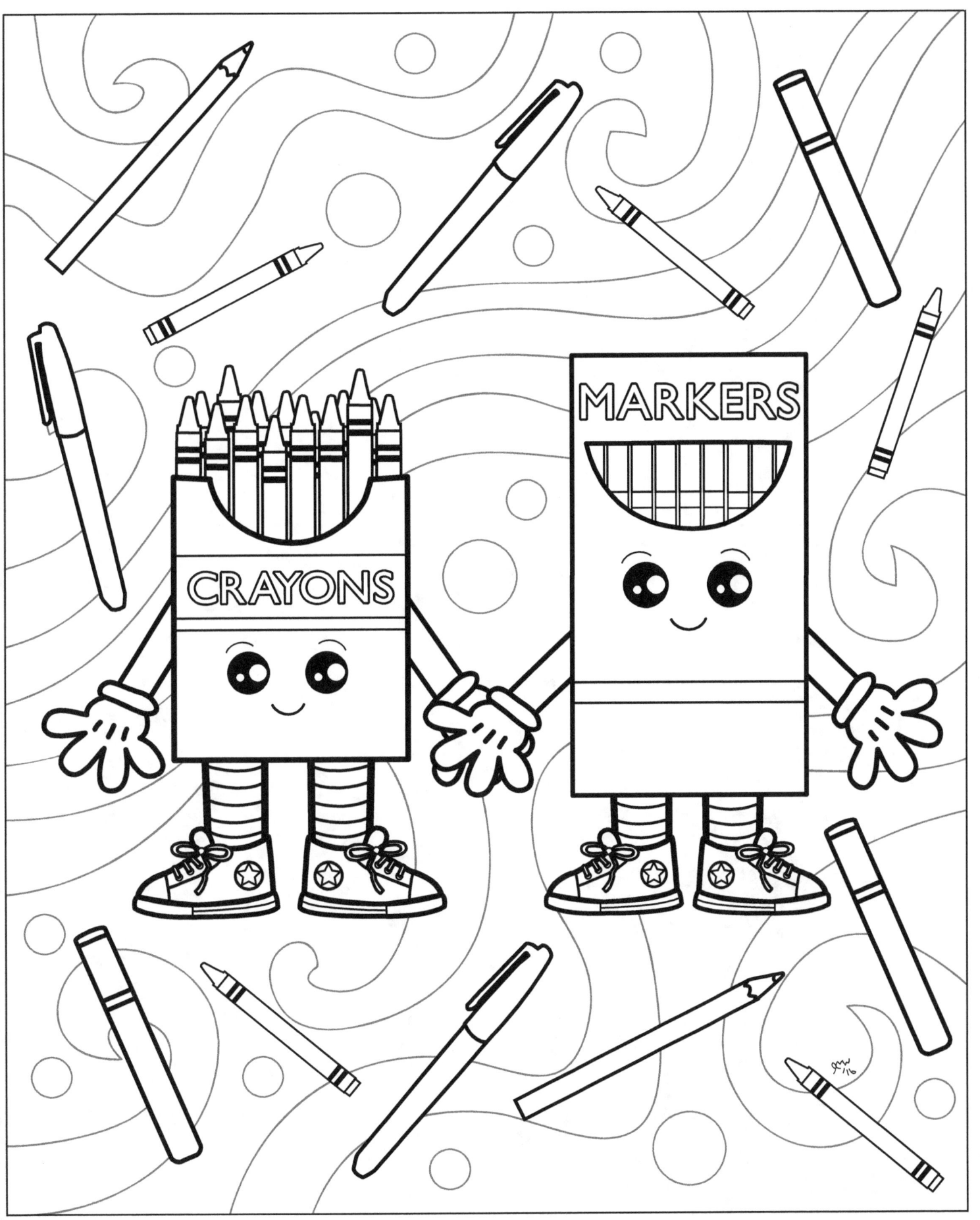

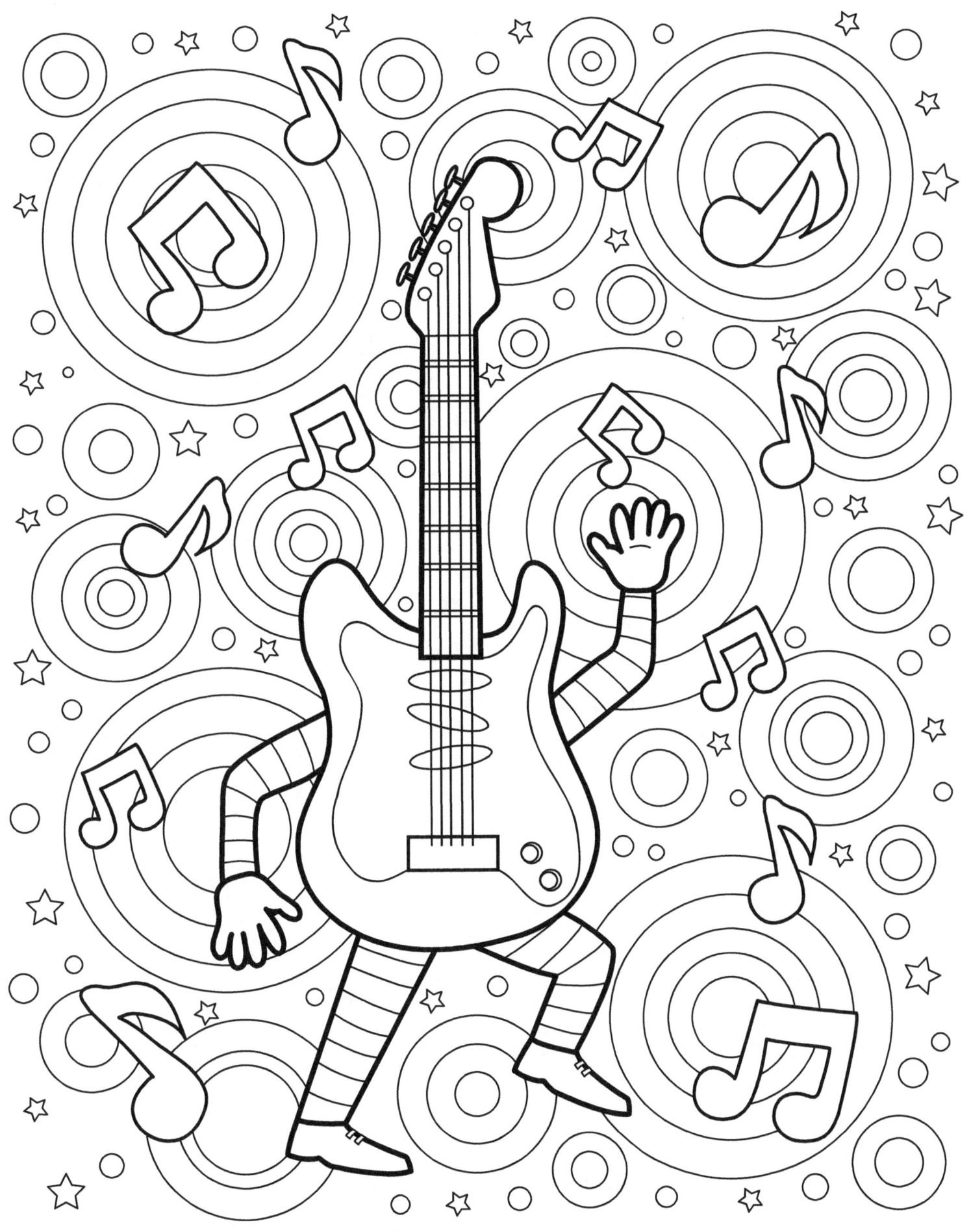

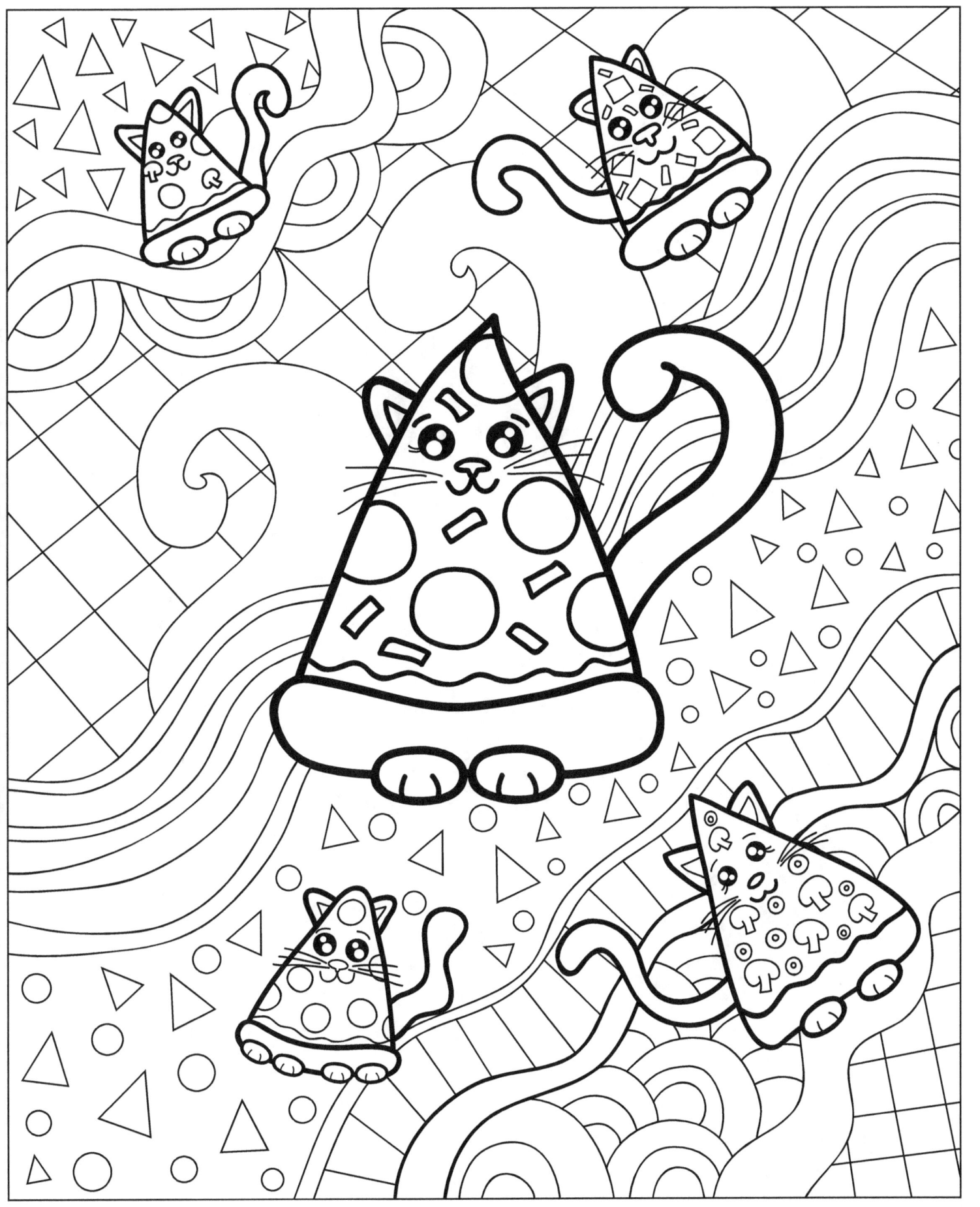

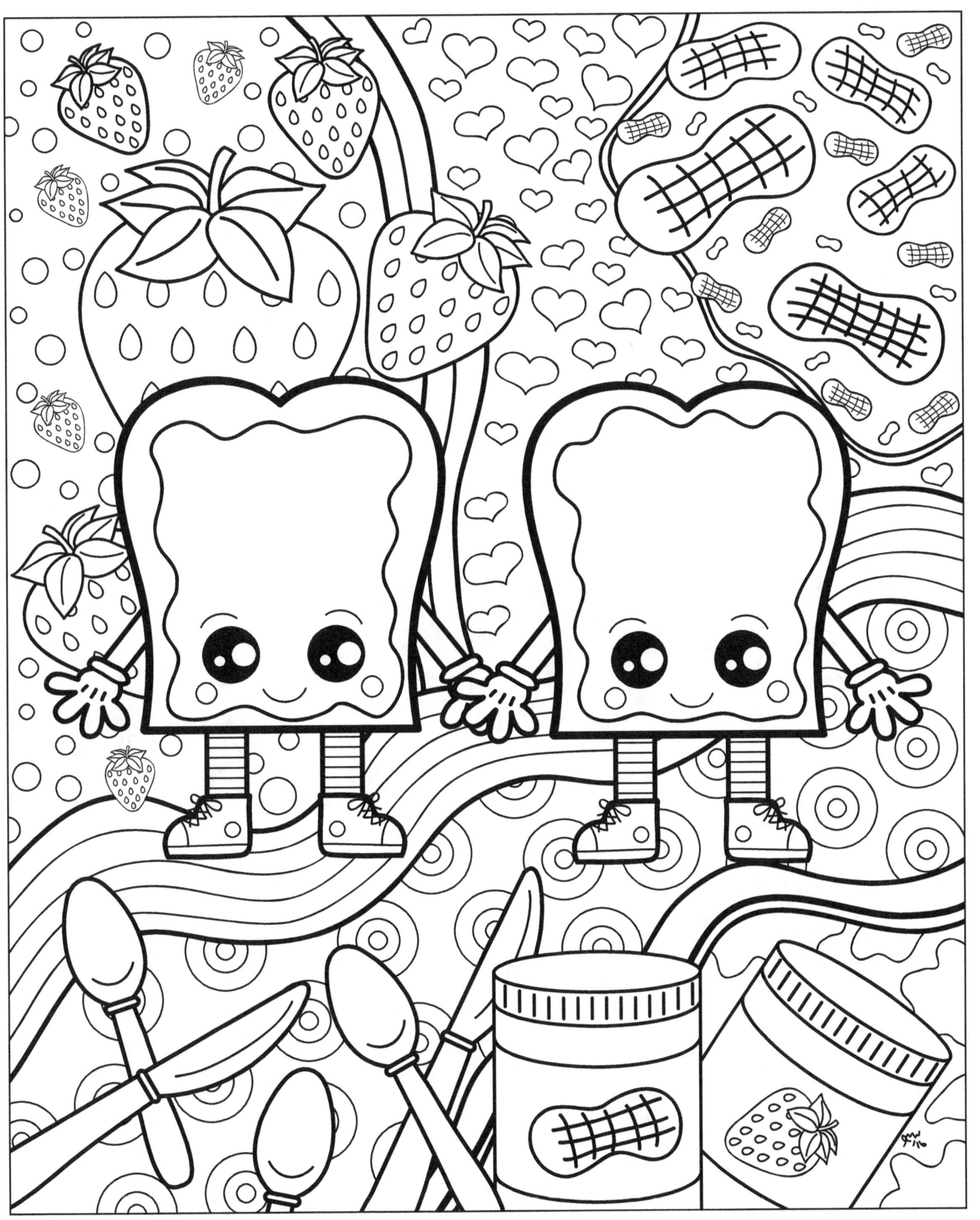

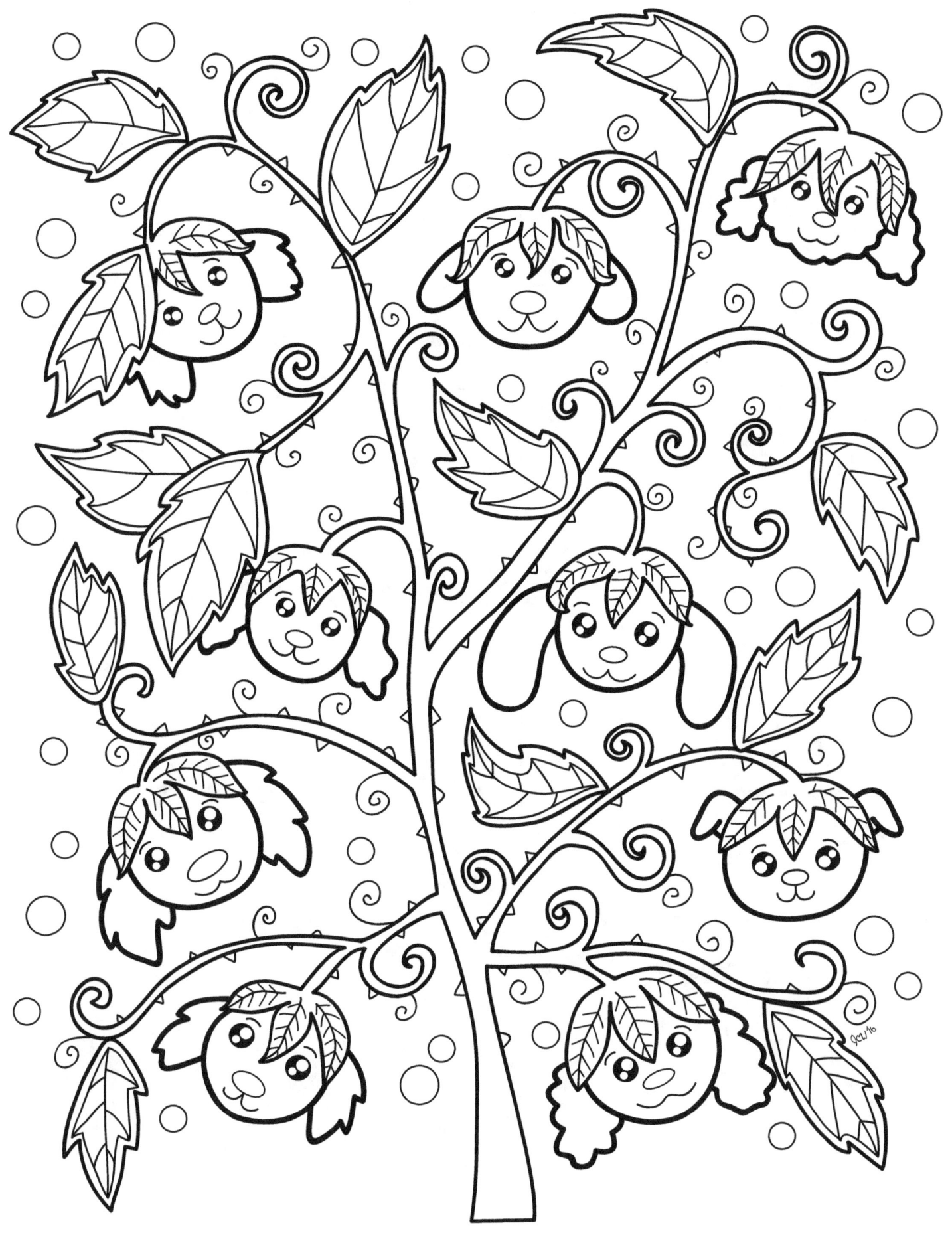

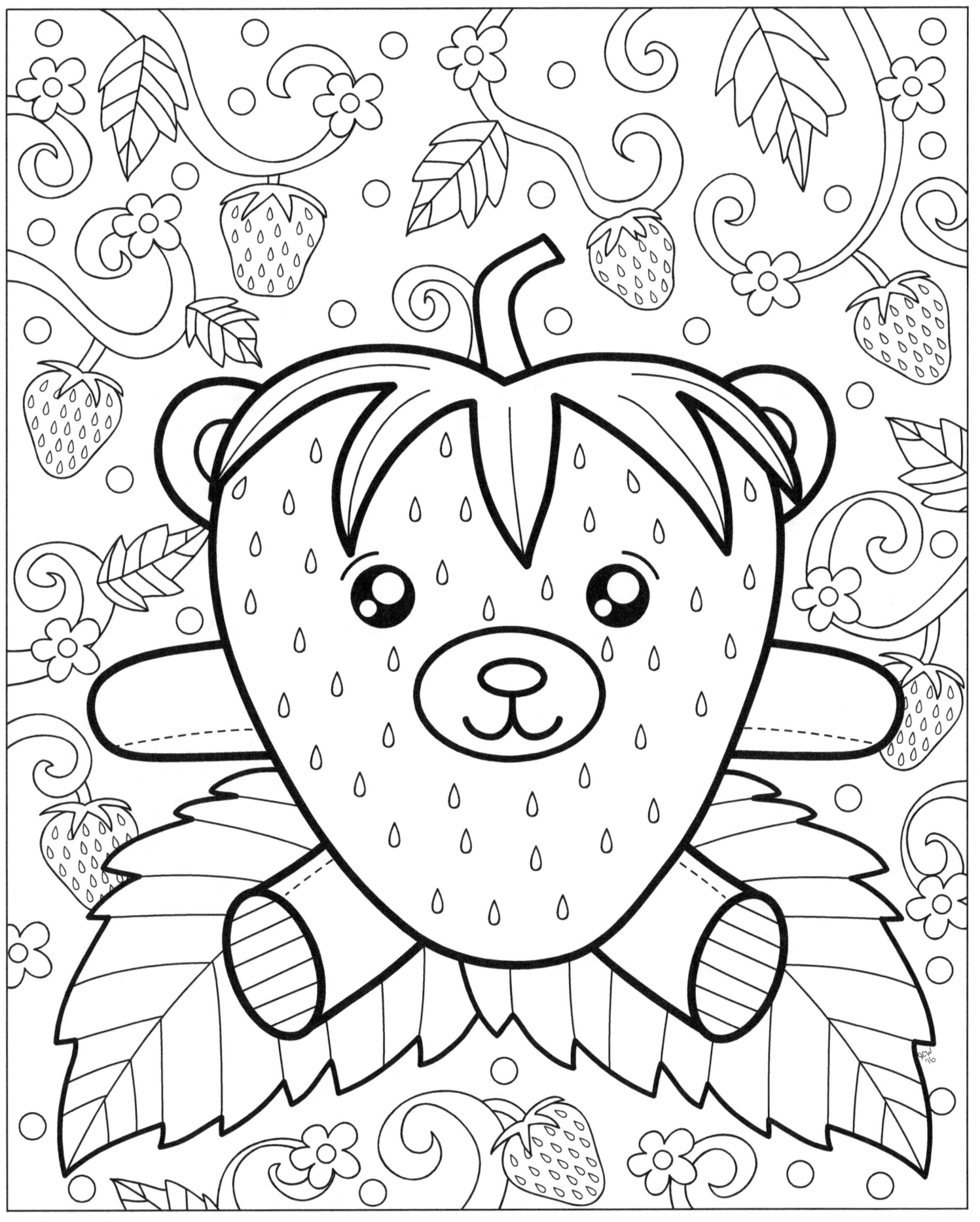

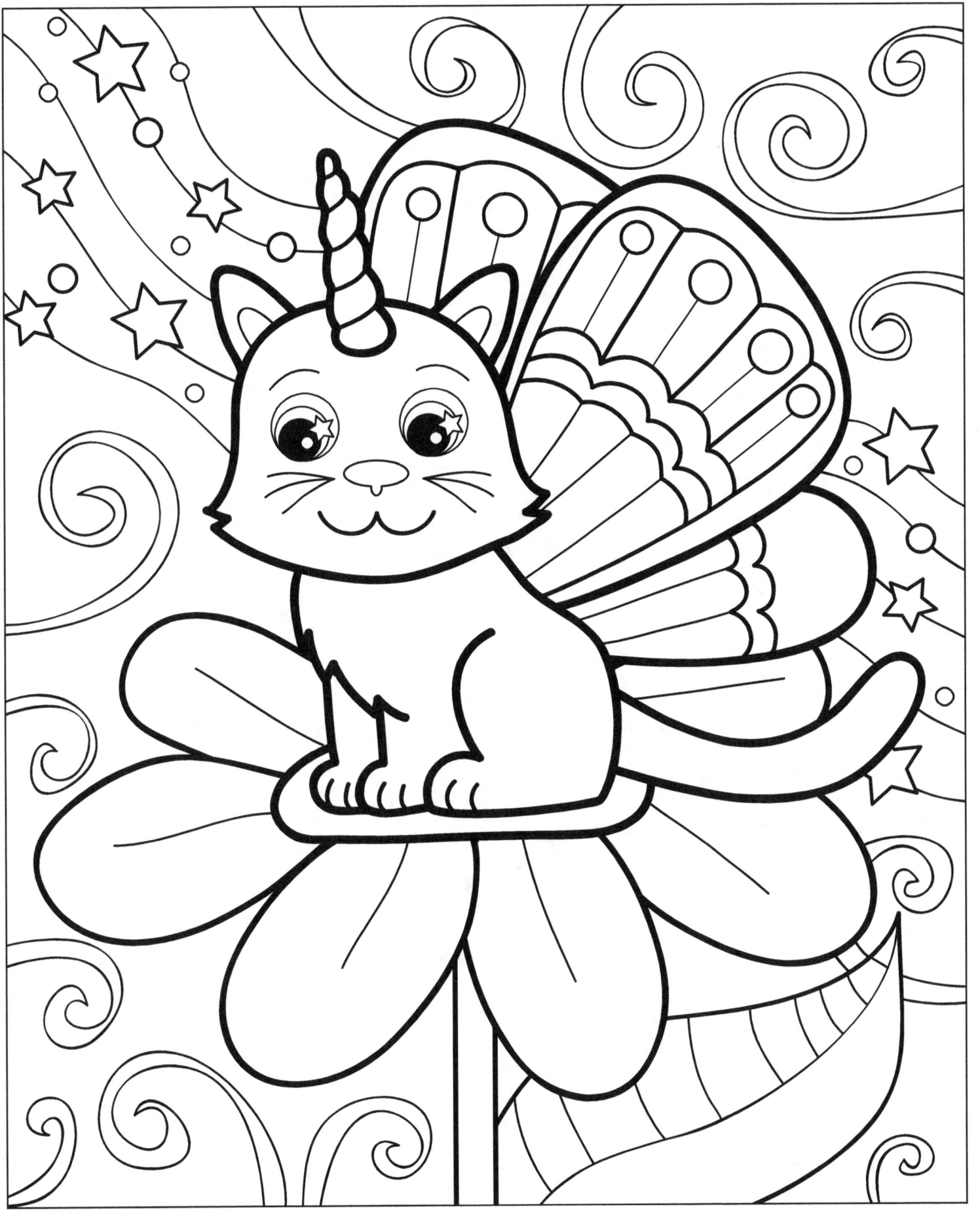

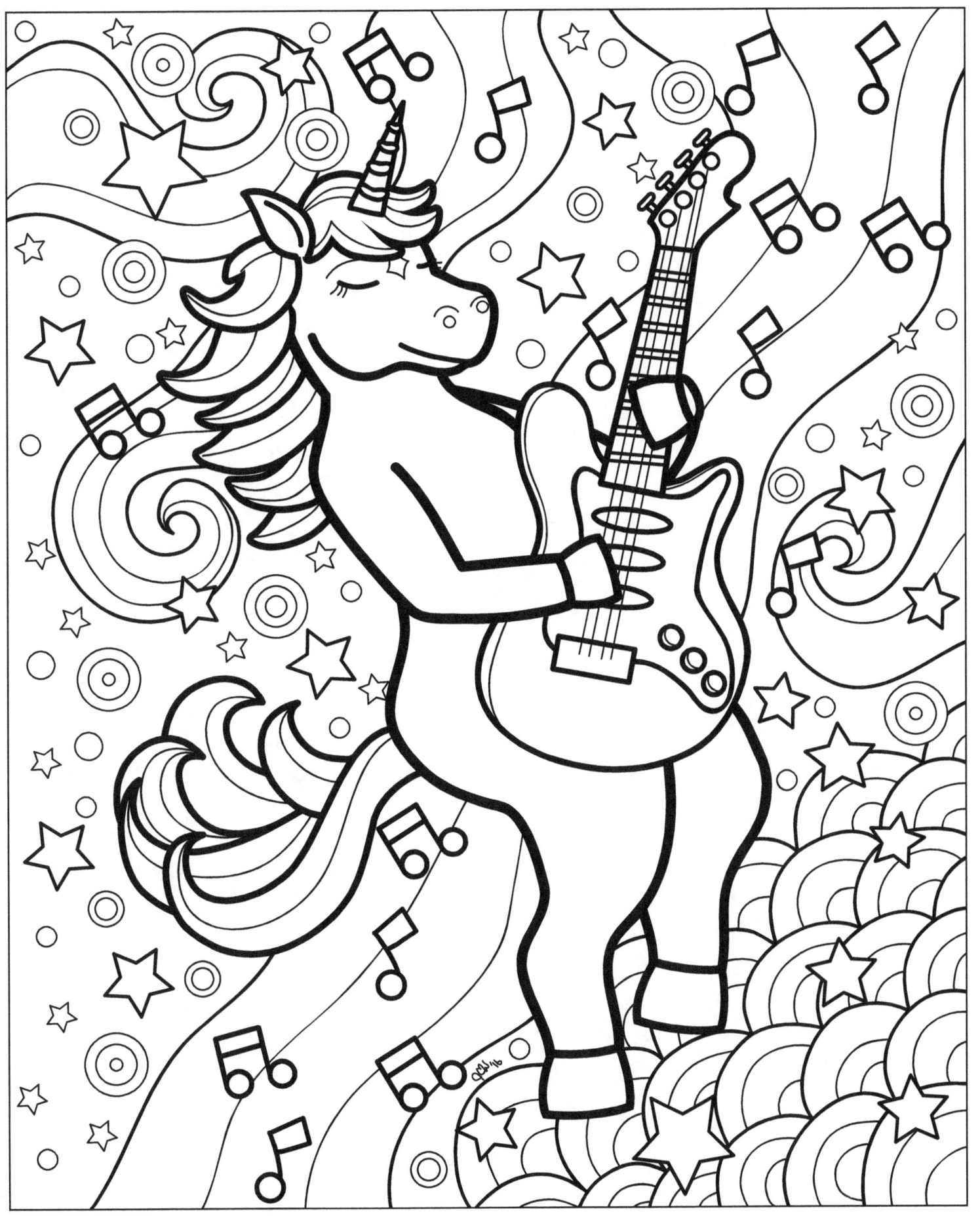

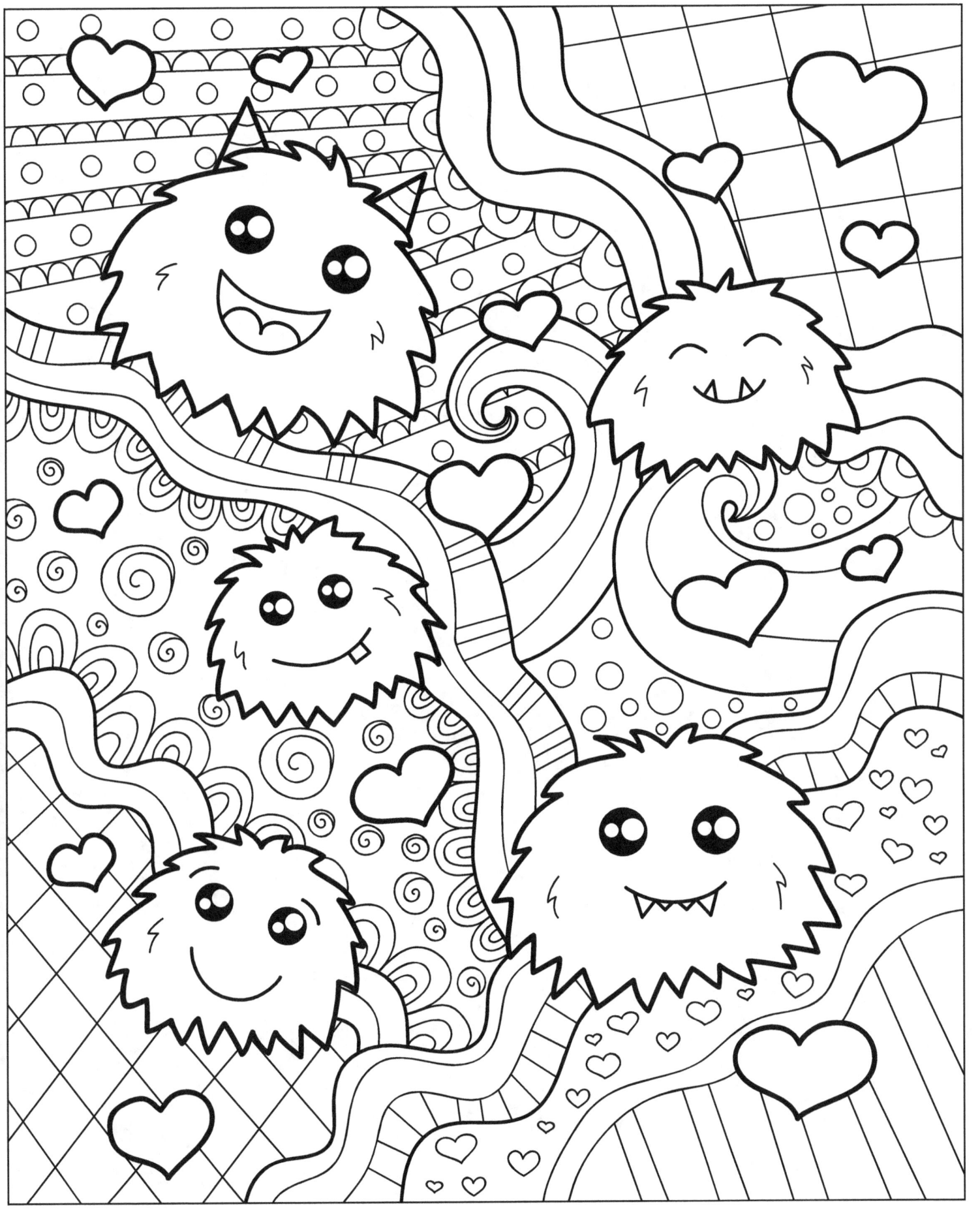

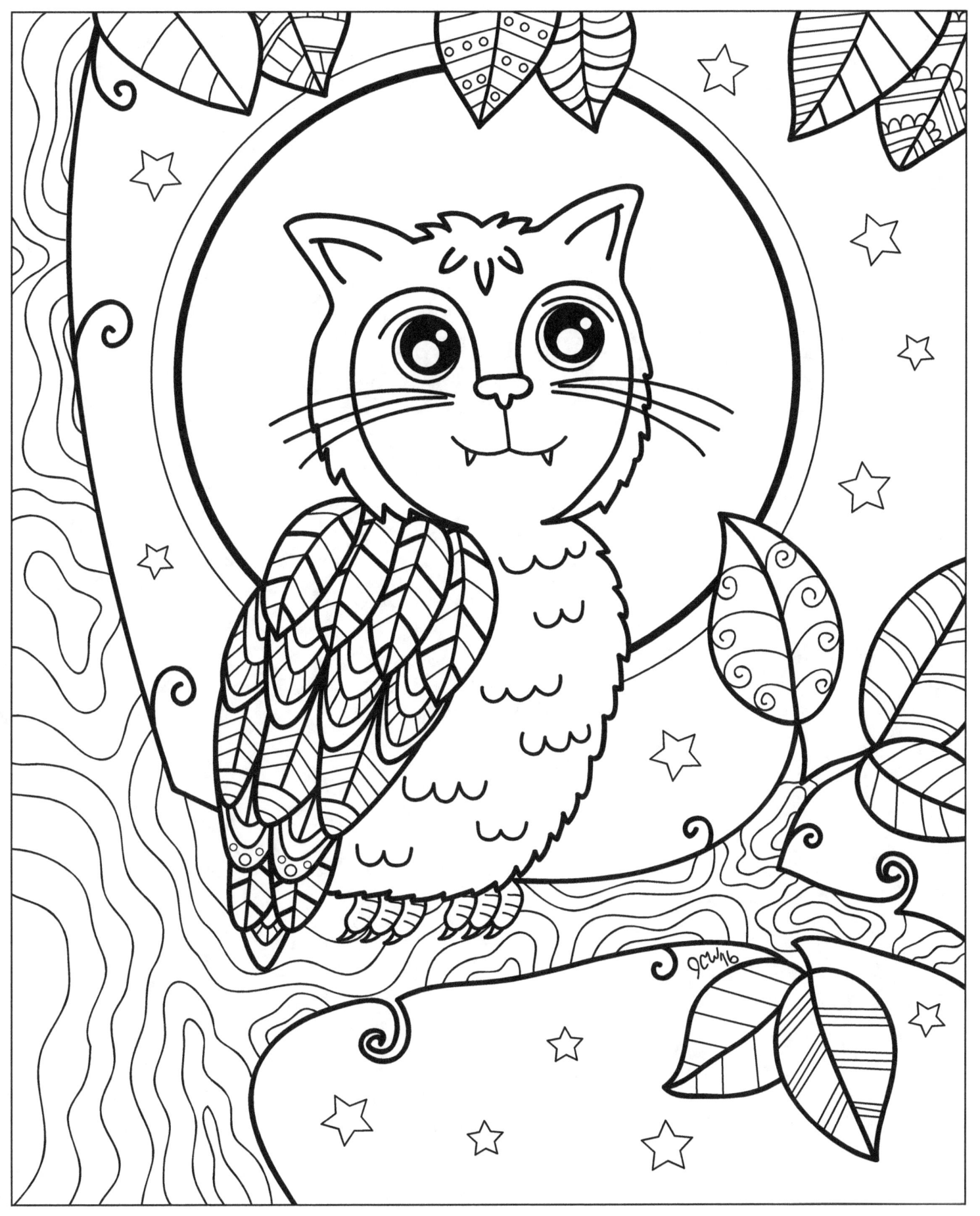

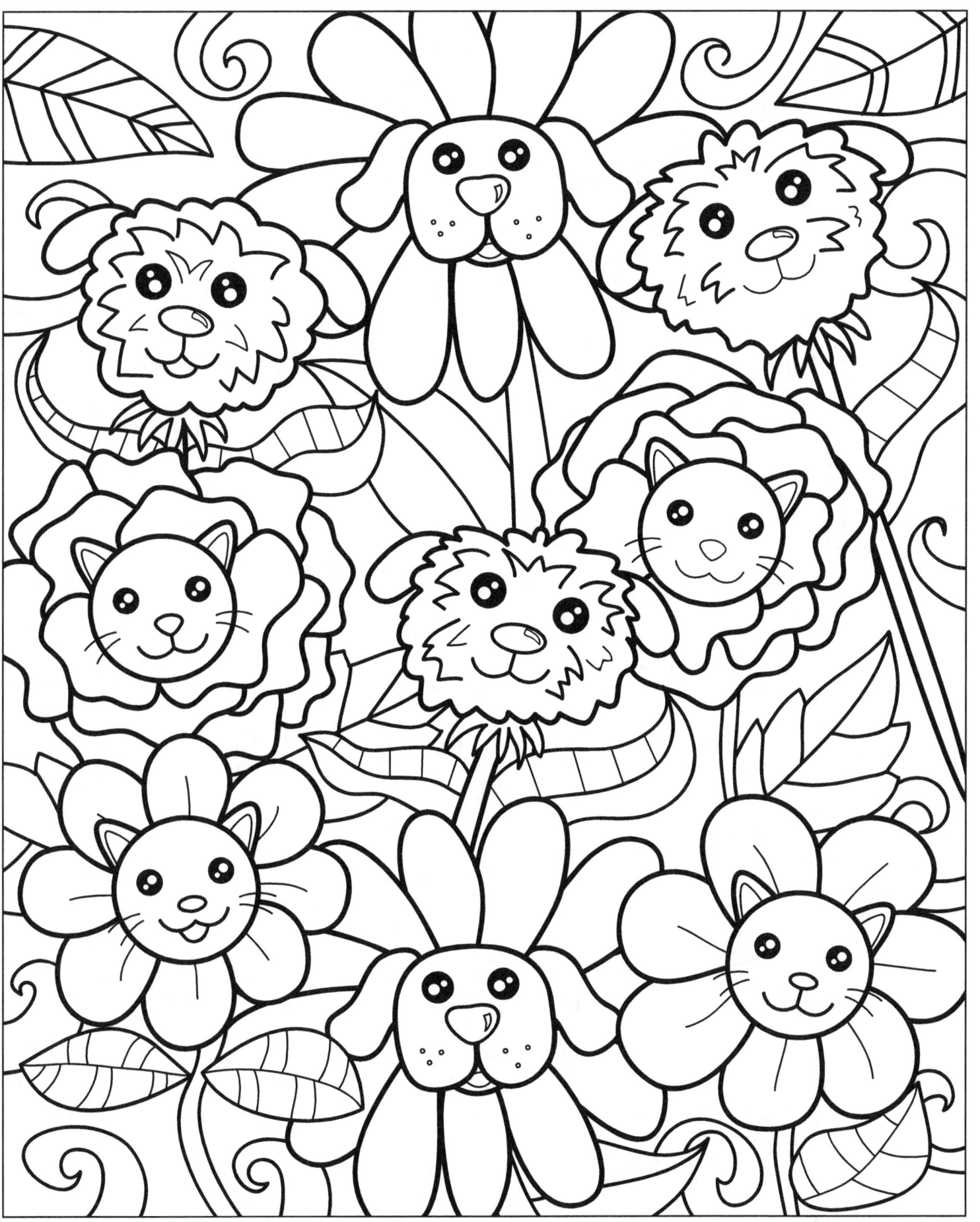

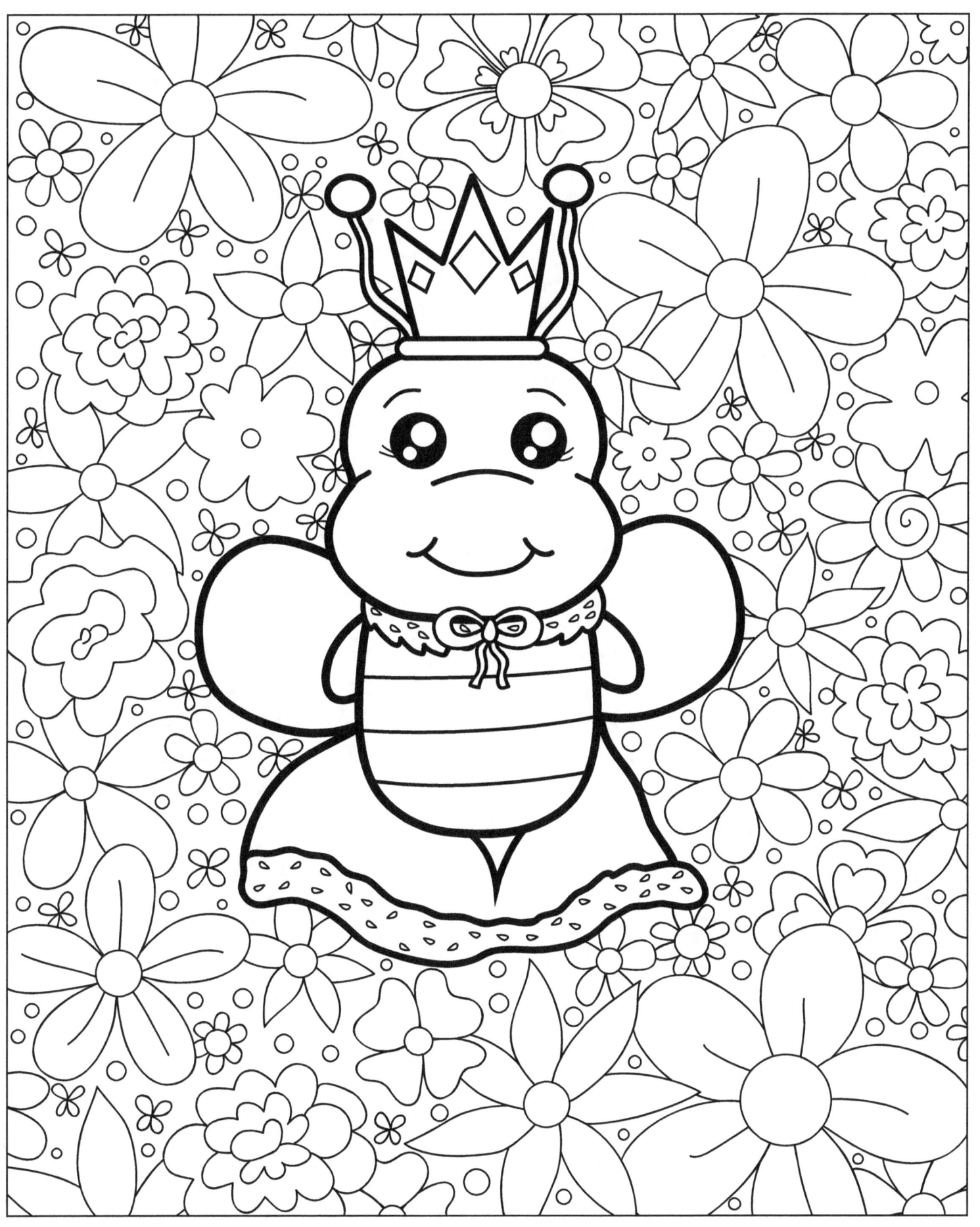

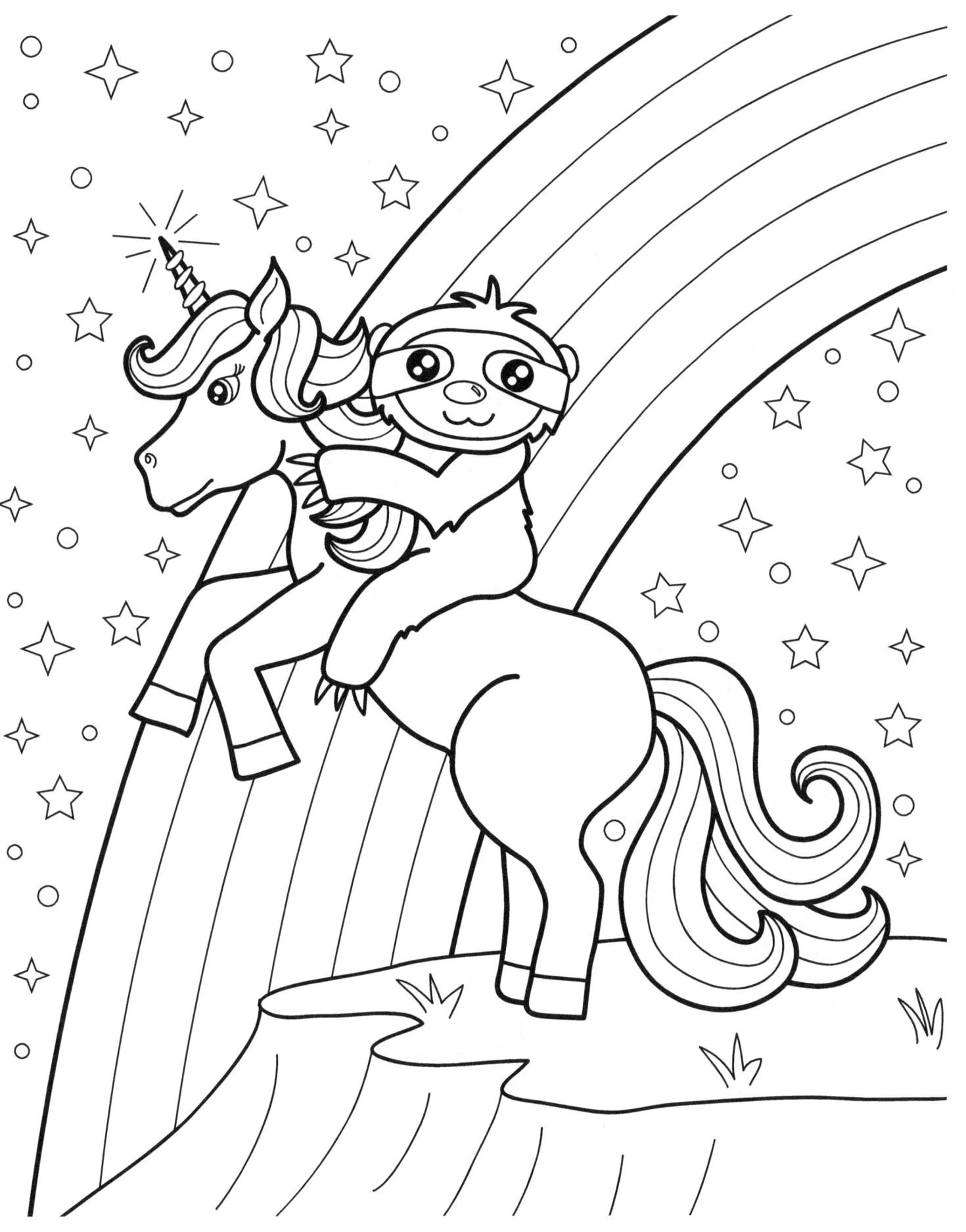

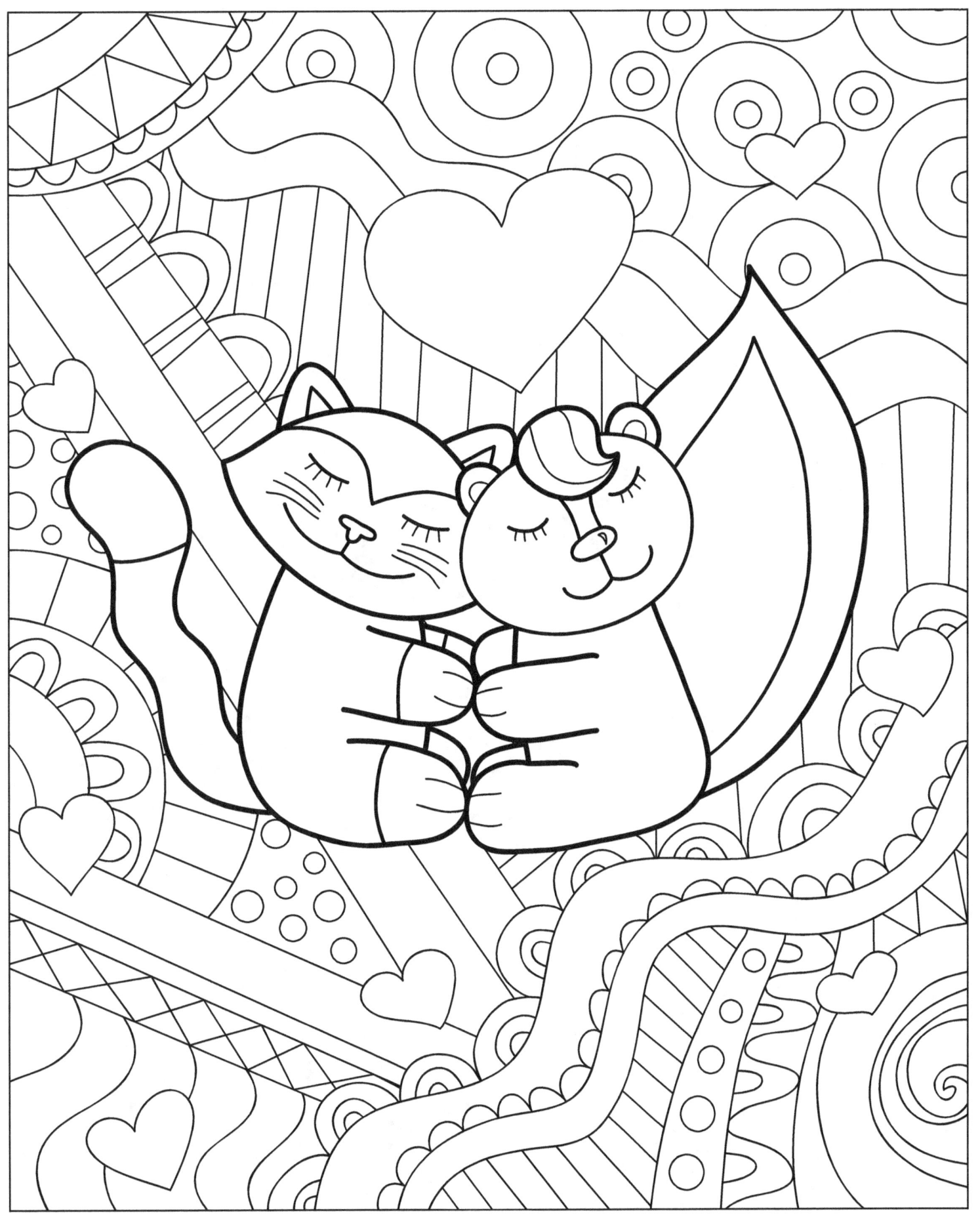

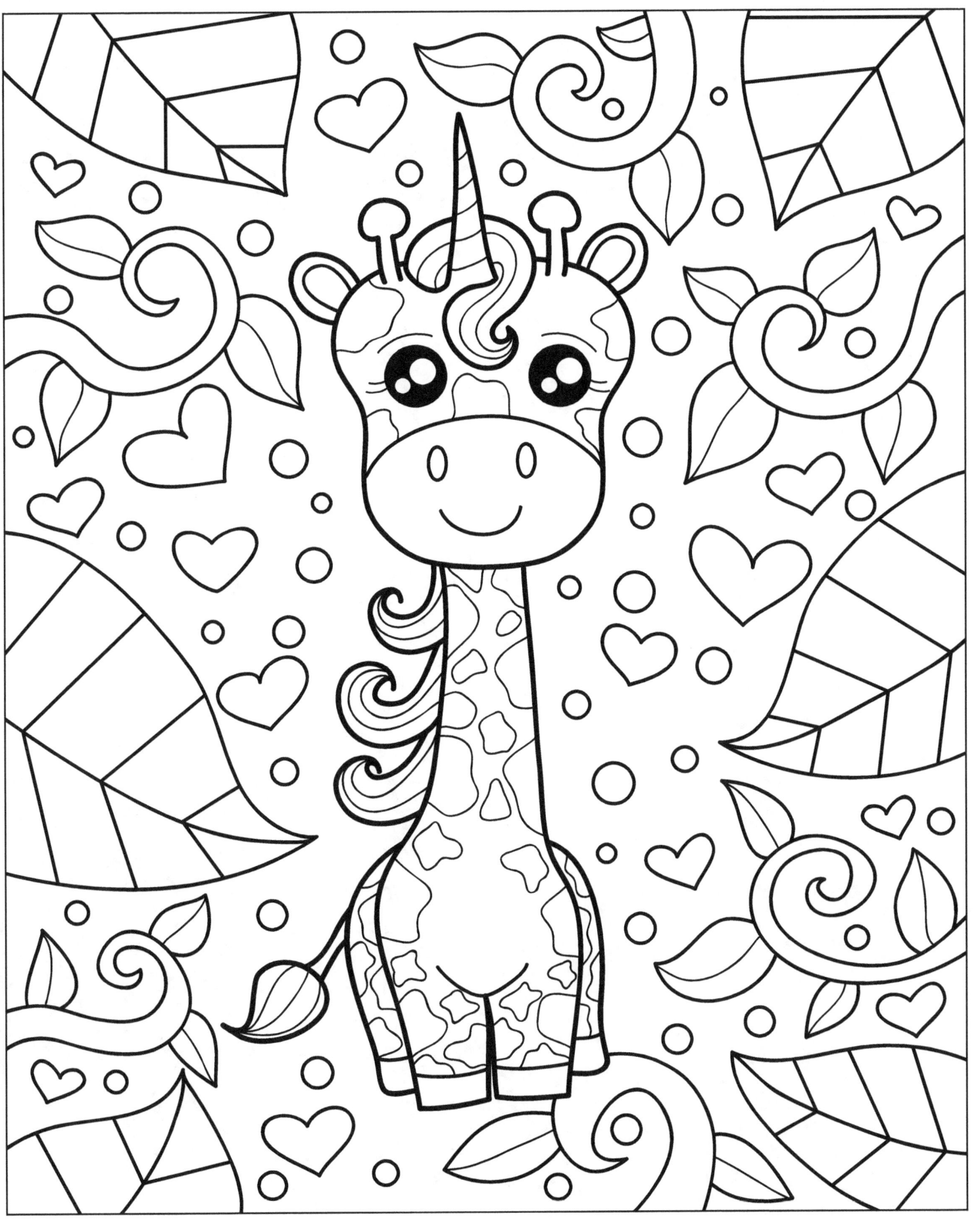

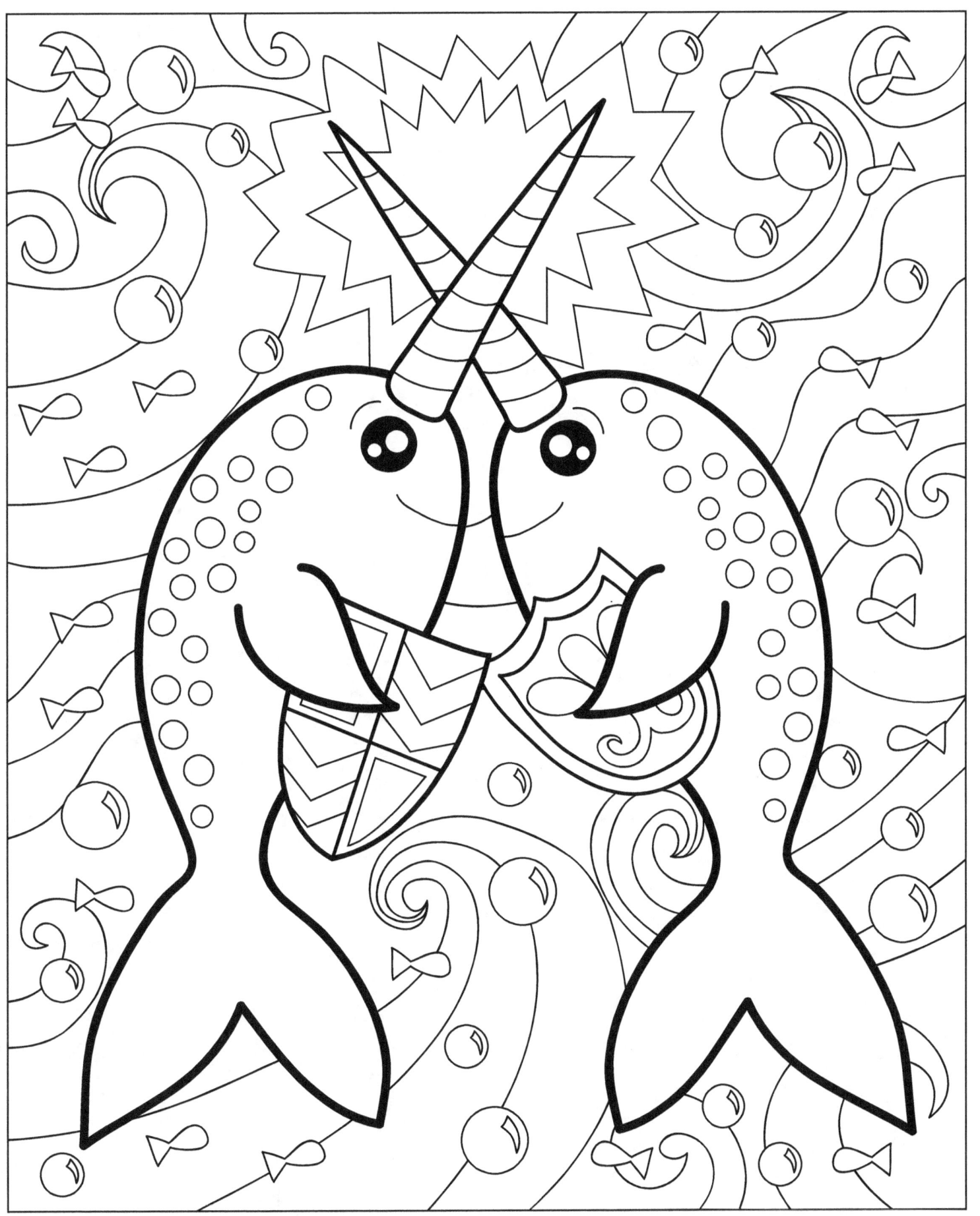

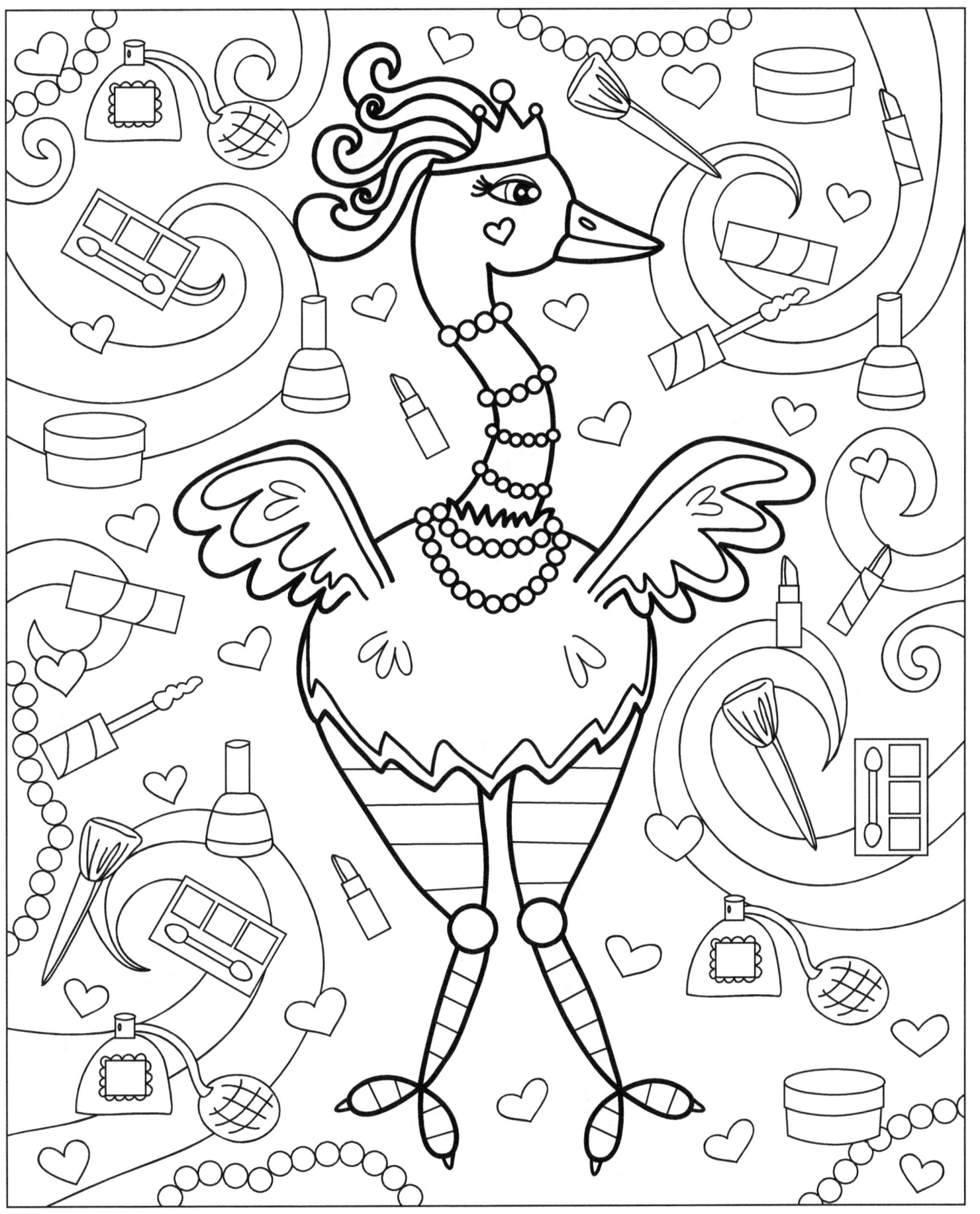

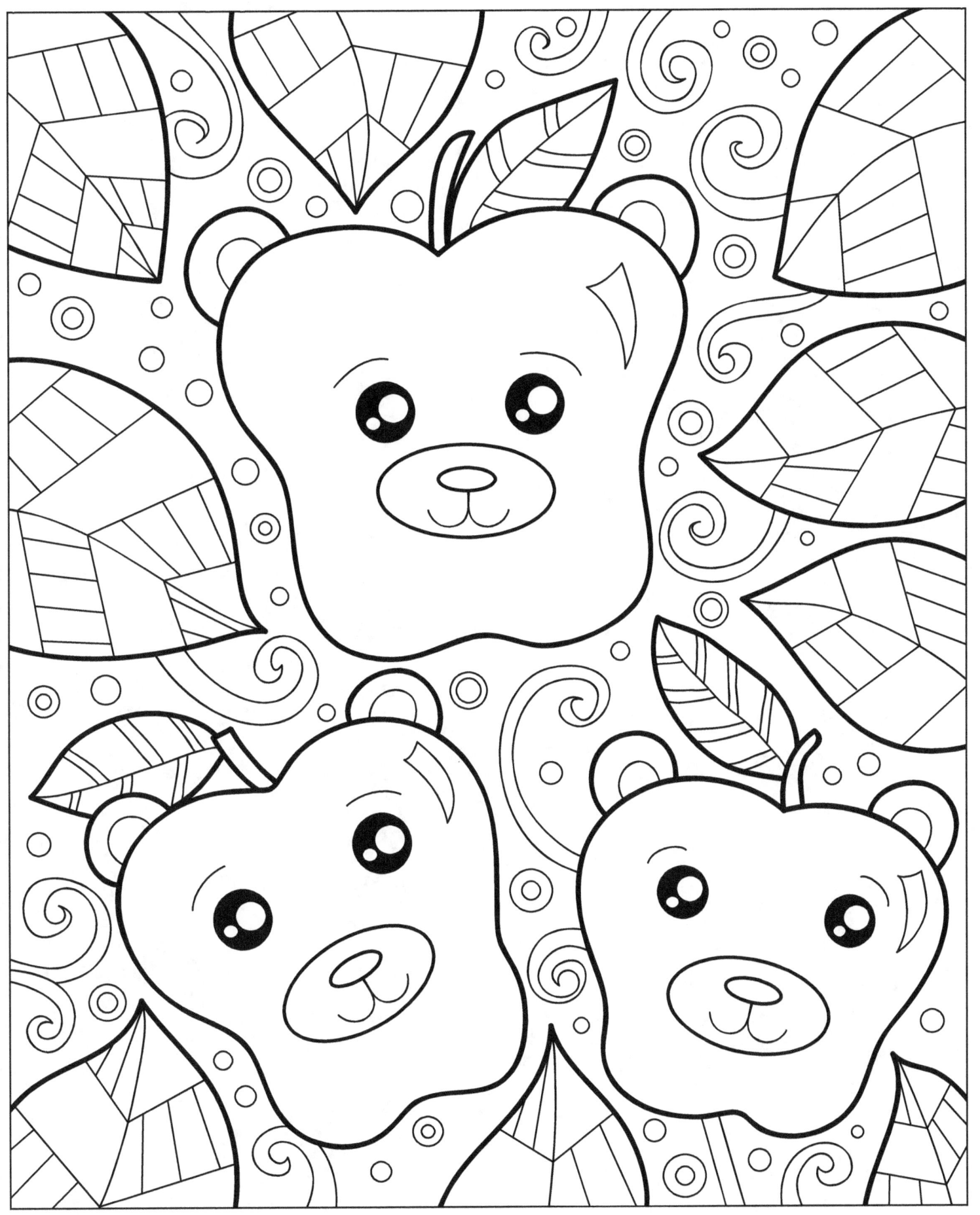

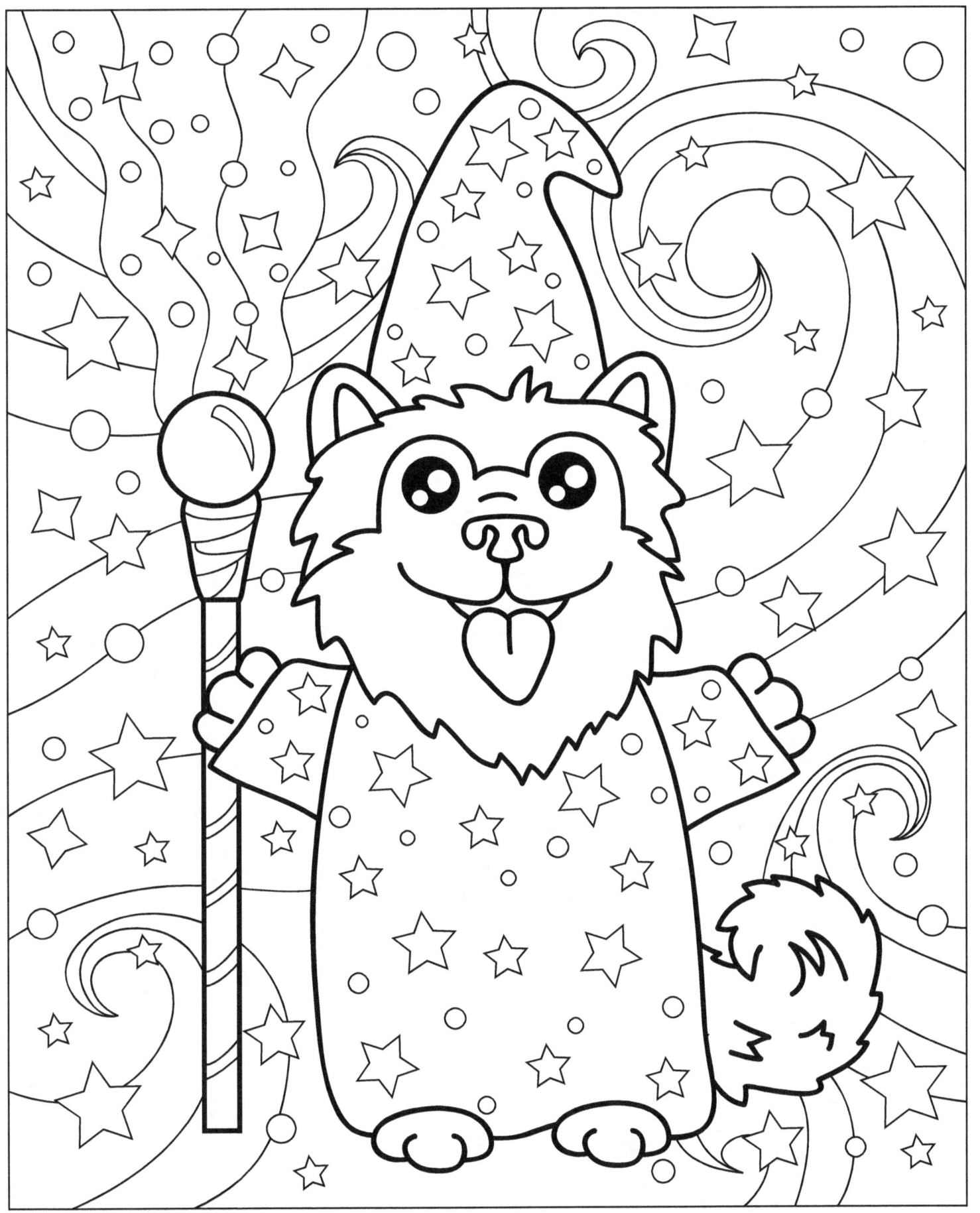

Check out my other books and more on Amazon and Etsy, and www.TheRootsOfDesign.com

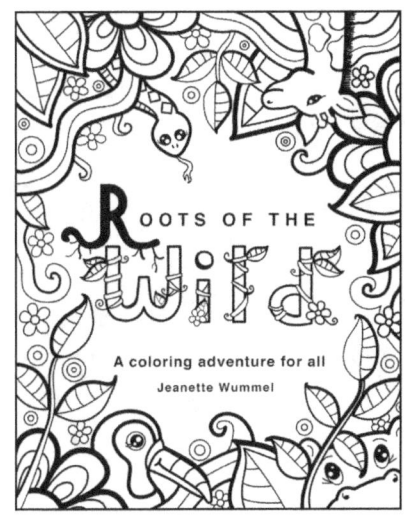
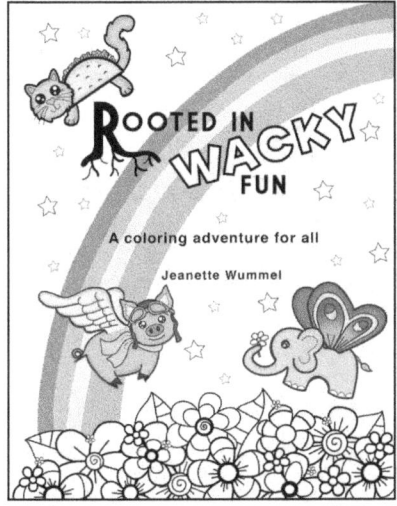
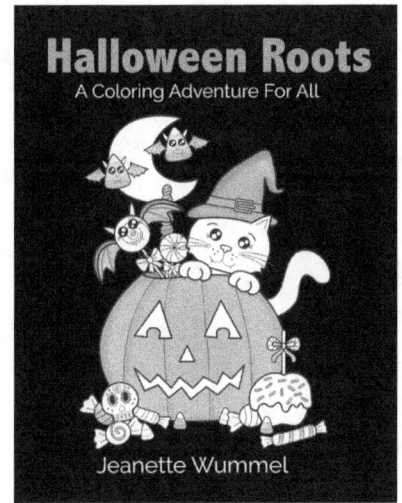
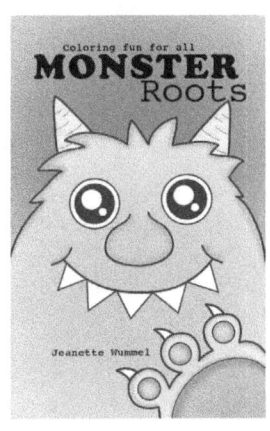
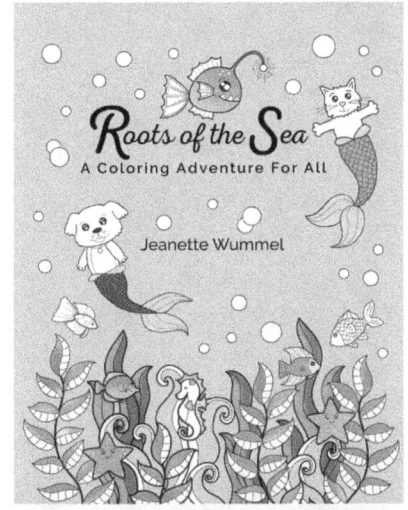
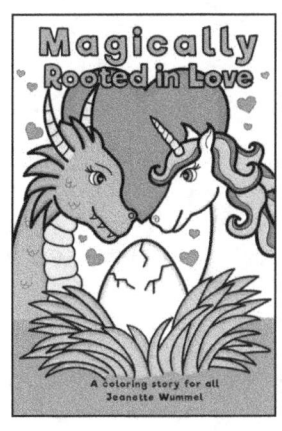
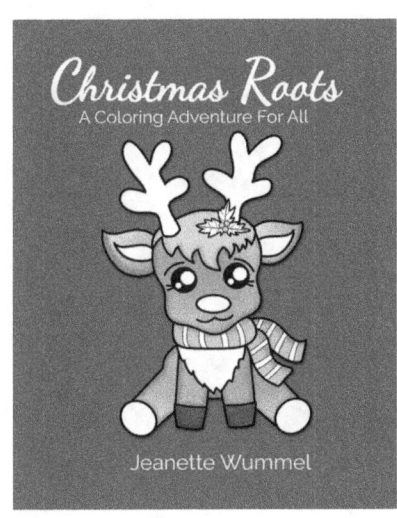
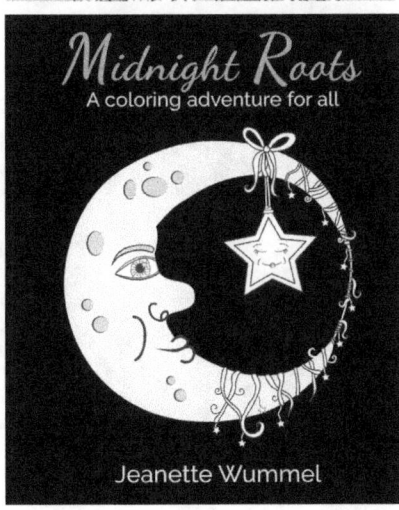
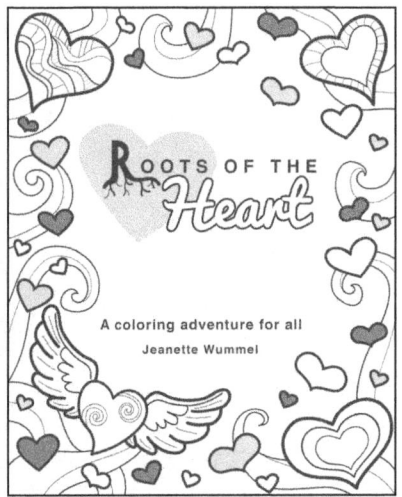